Produced by

EVENLEY RESIDENTS ASSOCIATION

The stories of two individuals,
Cicely Spencer and Bill Buggins
of the changes in the village in
the 20th century

Also published by Evenley Residents Association

ASPECTS OF EVENLEY

The history of Evenley, a small village in
Northamptonshire, from pre Roman times
to the present day

ISBN No. 0-9543808-1-9

Produced by Robert Boyd, Printing and Publishing Services
260 Colwell Drive, Witney, Oxon. OX28 5LW
From artwork supplied by Evenley Residents Association

SPONSORS

We would particularly like to thank our Sponsors for their generous donations which have made a major contribution to covering the costs of the publication of this book.

David & Barbara Bailey
Simon & Nicola Biltcliffe
Tim Boswell MP
Andrew & Mary Bullock
Chris & Marian Chippendale
Jessica Church
Bob & Janet Cropley
Evenley Parish Council
Evenley Village Shop
Stuart & Wendy Freestone
Andrew & Sally Gordon-Stewart
Jeremy & Josceline Hebblethwaite
Andreas & Philippa Heumann
HFC Consulting
Tony & Margaret Hollis
Roy & Julia Jennings

Ian & Liza Moodie
Old Hall Bookshop
John & Carolyn Oley
Kevin & Carrie O'Regan
Susan Parker
Lyn Pyatt & Neal Umney
Brian & Myrtle Robbins
The Red Lion, Evenley
Stephen Reid
Euan Spencer
Steven Spencer
Tony & Joyce Stevens
Richard & Terry Stopford
Michael & Liz Anne Wainwright
Walford & Round, Brackley
Chris & Emma Wightman

Evenley Cricket Club SNCC Premier League Champions 2005

ACKNOWLEDGEMENTS

We are extremely grateful to all those in Evenley and elsewhere who have helped with and contributed to the preparation and publication of this book and specifically to:

1. Stephen Reid for permission to publish his grandmother's letter to him and for providing many photographs.

2. Leslie Buggins for permission to publish his father's memoir 'Life was Like That' and for providing many photographs.

3. Susan Parker for providing many photographs of the Spencer family.

4   The Oxfordshire County Council Photographic Archive for kind permission to use the photographs of old Evenley from the Packer Collection.

5   The Northamptonshire Record Office for kind permission to use photographs of old Evenley and Brackley.

6. The Banbury Library and the Banbury Guardian for permission to use a photograph from their archives.

CONTENTS

LIST OF ILLUSTRATIONS

LIST OF ILLUSTRATIONS (CONT)

Note i: Reproduced by kind permission of Oxford County Council Photographic Archive.

Note ii: Reproduced by kind permission of Northamptonshire Record Office.

INTRODUCTION

After producing "Aspects of Evenley" in 2002 we are now publishing two memoirs about the past of the village; a letter from Cicely Spencer to her grandson describing her life and times in the village and secondly a broader perspective over a longer period by Bill Buggins.

Cicely Spencer and Bill Buggins were cornerstones of Evenley's history. Their memories of life in the village throughout the 20th century give us a very personal insight into rural life and the enormous changes it went through from their very different viewpoints.

The Old Manor, where Cicely Spencer spent the greater part of her life and where she brought up her four children, was dated about 1580. She bought the house in 1939 and lived there for nearly 50 years until she moved to Manor Cottage which she built next door and where she died in 1999.

Bill Buggins was born and bred in Evenley and lived much of his life at No. 5 Dormer Row, one of the cottages forming part of the original Evenley Hall estate and where his son, Leslie, still lives.

These two remarkable people have given us the legacy of their writings. They paint for us vivid pictures of Evenley and its inhabitants and describe how their lives and the village itself were changed for ever by two world wars, industrialisation, communications and politics.

We are privileged to be able to draw together these two complementary and historic memoirs into one book which we hope will be of interest to future generations of Evenley residents, just as much as to those who live here today.

Our gratitude goes to Stephen Reid, Cicely's grandson and Leslie Buggins, Bill Buggins's son, for permission to reprint these stories just as they were written.

LETTER FROM STEPHEN REID
ABOUT HIS GRANDMOTHER
CICELY SPENCER

What a lovely surprise! Thank you so much for your fascinating book "Aspects of Evenley". I lived with my Grandmother Cicely Spencer (known to all of us as "Omi") at the Old Manor for about a year when aged 7 and even attended the village school for a short while where I remember being made to stand in the corner on at least one occasion! This would have been about 1960—I think it closed down not long afterwards. Eleanor Tetley was Omi's mother so the house had been in the family quite a long time even then. She moved there when her marriage broke up but at the age of 80 she decided it was all a bit much for her and so had built Manor Cottage (for which the original village quarry was reopened so that it blended in with the old buildings). When she moved to Manor Cottage she took two fixtures with her—(1) the old cast iron bath and (2) a dim blue "blackout" light bulb which had been installed in the upstairs loo in 1939. This latter continues to function perfectly, and when she died aged 97 it was left to me and is now installed in one of our loos where the children still leave it on regularly, despite which mistreatment it continues to survive—it has been in continuous use now for over 60 years.

By all means please do publish Omi's entire letter in your next book. I would be delighted to see it more widely read and appreciated, as she was a very special person.

I shall much enjoy reading your book and I am sure it will bring back many happy memories. My only regret is that Omi is not alive to see it—though I am sure that somehow she will know of it.

Stephen Reid

Stephen Reid aged two at the gate of the Manor

Cicely Spencer

CICELY SPENCER'S LETTER

TO HER GRANDSON

STEPHEN REID

My dear grandson Stephen,

You have always urged me to write my memories of the family so I will tell you about Evenley, which you always loved and, as a little boy, the house fascinated you.

About the year 1930 your great grandmother, Eleanor Mary Tetley, was looking for a home for herself and her daughter, Mace Caroline Wynn Tetley, hereafter known as Wuppy. They had a rented cottage in Brigstock where there was an old gardener called John Walton. He said to my mother "you go and look in Evenley (where he came from) you'll find a home there". My mother went to look and there she saw and fell in love with the Old Manor. It was in a very derelict state as it had not been inhabited for three years. There was no electric light; water—a village supply—was pumped by hand. The walls Wuppy described as looking like Stilton cheese. The garden was a wilderness of brambles and elders. It was to let for sixty pounds a year—my mother offered one pound a week and said she would put in electric light—and so it was agreed!

Omi on a donkey with Wuppy

5

The electricity was installed with lots of points on the four floors for £17.10s.0d and my mother, who never had much money, had a motto "never spoil the ship for a ha'porth of tar" so set about having the house decorated from top to bottom by a London firm. The foreman said it took him three days trying to work out how to tackle the job. The house was built about 1580. The original staircase was made using two great limbs of trees and steps put where it was easy to fix them, no steps were exactly the same, some deeper than others, some higher. I suppose it was a dreadful thing to do but I had a new main staircase made, though two of the branches are still to be seen in the cupboard under the stairs. One of my uncles, when staying with my mother, actually fractured his skull falling on those stairs.

The Manor

In 1939 Wuppy became engaged to Stephen Renshaw, my mother moved to a flat in Oxford and the Old Manor was up for sale. A this time I was looking for a new home for myself and my children and I thought it would be a good idea to buy the house as we already felt at home there, having often stayed with my mother and the children spending their half terms there. We moved in on the 1st June 1939 on a hot day with the tar in the road soft which got on the shoes of the furniture removers and from there onto the new carpets!

The village was just coming to the end of the old fashioned way things had been for a very long time with a Squire at Evenley Hall who owned all the cottages and employed many of the men to work on the land or in the garden and stables. Other local men worked on the railway—they rode their bicycles to work. In the evenings they cultivated their allotments and the vegetables they grew were "half their keep" as one man told me. There were large families as often the girl married the boy next door, or at least someone in the village, making big family connections and the children went to the village school and home to their mothers for their dinners. On Sundays the men and boys who could sing were in surplices in the church choir. The church bells were rung and old customs were still observed, for instance on the 1st of May the school children went round the village carrying a garland of flowers and sang songs and there was always a bonfire on the green on November 5th.

There was no sanitation in the cottages only an earth closet at the end of the garden. When it had to be emptied the allotments came in useful and they certainly produced excellent vegetables! When we came the wells were still in use although the Squire had put standpipes for some of the cottages. There was a supply of water pumped by a windmill from where the Old Manor had its water. It was then pumped by hand to a storage tank in the attic.

I remember one night Mrs. Brown, who lived in my cottage across the road and whose husband was away at the war, was about to have a baby. Her parents woke me up to send for the doctor - "our Moira's bad". I rang the doctor then didn't feel I could just go back to bed so dressed and went to her. For some reason the nurse did not arrive and I had to assist the doctor. I remember washing something by moonlight at one of the standpipes. I was in the room when the doctor said, after the baby was born and handed to me, "there's another Mrs. Brown" and poor Mrs. Brown said "not another doctor". They were both boys and premature and sadly they died. I said afterwards one really should have training in midwifery if one lived in a village! I did feel very battered after this experience.

There was a small shop and carrier—a man with a horse and cart who would do shopping for the villagers once a week—and a muffin man who came round with a basket on his head, ringing a bell, selling crumpets and muffins.

Another custom was to make home made wine - elderberry, dandelion,

7

cowslip, parsley and many others. How delicious they were and very potent too. It was a form of hospitality to offer a glass of wine. You will remember the elderflower wine I made, always very popular with you and David.

The men of the village brought the best of their vegetables for the Harvest Festival. Sadly that is no longer the case, fewer and fewer people grow their own vegetables. When I bought the allotments to save them being built on there was a waiting list to have a piece—now many of them are unused.

Many visitors at the Old Manor looked forward to the peace of the countryside only to be roused in the early morning by crowing cockerels! A sound not heard today.

When there was a funeral, the coffin was taken to the church on a bier—a long flat carriage on wheels which was pulled by hand—with the family walking behind. When my mother saw one of these processions from her bedroom window she said that was how she wanted to go as she had a great dislike of hearses. She was staying with me during her last illness and I made sure her wish was fulfilled. She died at the end of January and I wished we could have postponed the funeral for a few days - little did I know that was the start of the coldest part of the winter I ever remember.

Eleanor Mace Tetley

The first thing to freeze up at the Old Manor was the central heating. Rosemary, Steven and Euan had all left home by then and Sue was away at school. I remember my bath for many weeks was just a basin in front of the sitting room fire and I must have cooked on that fire because the boiler in the kitchen was frozen up. I had a second hand Austin and if I did go out in it I had to drain the radiator each time, anti-freeze was only just coming into use and was not considered good for the engine! I had that car for seventeen years—it's number was XS 4636. It was a well known car. One day I rang up the Top Station in Brackley (there were two stations in the town in those days) to ask the time of a train and the clerk at the booking office said "That's Mrs. Spencer isn't it - well do you know your car is up here? One of the family had used it to get to the station! On a trip to London we handed in our car keys at the booking office and on our return the clerk collecting the tickets handed them back to us!

Cicely with Steve, Rosemary and Euan

This reminds me of another story which shows how small our world was at that time. Long, long before you could dial a number there was a man at the Exchange to whom you gave the number you wanted and he would get it for you. At one time there was a one armed man working the Exchange and if I was going out at night I would ring him and tell him where I would be. We had some friends in Turweston whose name was Bradshaw and the eldest of the family was Caroline, a great friend of

Susan's. One day someone asked for the Bradshaws' number and was told "It's no good ringing that number Mrs. Bradshaw is hunting and the General has gone to London!

To go back to 1939, after we were settled in I took my children and Sue's Nanny, Patsy, and we went off to Brittany with your Great Aunt Muriel and her only child Thyrza. After a time there were announcements over the wireless saying all British passport holders should go home. We stayed on and the English speaking holidaymakers disappeared. We thought we would move nearer to St. Malo as it was a port and booked ourselves into a hotel in Dinard. However, Muriel thought she should send her car back so we all went over to St. Malo, she to make arrangements for the car whilst the rest of us went sightseeing. When we were on the old walls we saw Thyrza hurrying up the road below us and shouted to her. She shouted back that we were to go home straight away as the last regular boat was sailing that night. We arrived at Southampton where there were Red Cross ships berthed and reached home on Thursday. War was declared on the Sunday, September 3rd which was to change forever the way of life we had all known.

The first problem to tackle was the blackout. We must not show even a glimmer of light from our windows because of German aircraft flying over at night to bomb Coventry and other cities. It was difficult with mullion windows as one could not fit the black material into the stone with drawing pins. That was why I bought a little blue electric bulb for the lavatory (not called loo in those days) so that the light would be dim. That little bulb is still in use in 1993. I remember meeting you off the school train at Victoria and your first words were "Is the blue light still working?" It would only have been a mere stripling of about twenty years at that time!

Blue Light Bulb

Now began a time of great difficulties. Shortage of food with such tiny rations for growing children, travelling difficulties with overcrowded trains, and with clothes it was "make do and mend" and there were no cleaners. Petrol was rationed and at one time we had none at all. Going to the dentist in Oxford was our outing of the holiday. Rosemary solved the problem by riding to Aynho, stabling the horse at the station and continuing by train.

Then there were the evacuees. One family called Blanchflower I still see occasionally and from whom I receive a Christmas card. Their mother went mad whilst they were with me because of the bombs and the doctor said I was responsible for her until she was certified and could go to an asylum in Northampton.

We had bombs close to the village which cracked the attic windows and gradually the ceilings came down. Cows were killed and there was structural damage to the cottages.

The Vicar and his wife felt rather isolated in the Vicarage as there were not other houses near them. They came and slept in the downstairs kitchen. She had a mattress on the floor and he managed with chairs. One night I said I would give them supper. There was a dreadful noise, they disappeared down the kitchen stairs and I shot up and picked Sue out of her cot. It was a landmine near the top of Bicester hill. My little dog, Twinkle, hid in the kitchen cupboard.

There is another little episode to do with the Vicar! One morning at the early service there was a long pause. I looked up wondering why the Vicar was silent. He stood by the altar with his glasses in his hand looking bewildered. I thought he must be ill. I tried to think if there was anyone in the congregation who had done their First Aid, then went up towards him followed by a young officer from Evenley Hall. There, standing at the altar rail, were two large dogs!

The boys, Steven and Euan, spent their holidays working on the Franklin's farm—meals had to be adjusted so that the tractor never stopped. After being at school at Bryanston Steve went to Loughborough College where he got a degree. He travelled on an old motorbike. On V.E. day, early in the morning, I heard a noise in the old kitchen—it was Steve and a friend, who had travelled pillion, arriving home through the kitchen window.

Rosemary became the age to be "called up". She could not join the ATS or the Wrens as there were no vacancies. I thought she should do something that would qualify her for a job after the war so she did a nursery training course and indirectly this is where you come into the story. One of my wartime jobs was having a pie shop in the back kitchen every Wednesday. This was a WVS job to help people with their rations—people in towns could have a meal "off the rations" at British restaurants. The pies were delivered by Joan Hobson and we became great friends. I always tried to have something for her elevenses like peanut butter, not rationed but difficult to get hold of. She was pregnant and wanted a nanny. Rosemary became that nanny and ultimately went to Germany with the Hobsons and there met your father.

I had many village jobs to do with the war—mostly collecting things. For example once a week I went round the village with a barrow and collected whatever could be spared from the gardens. A stick or two of rhubarb was a contribution from one old lady, and it was packed off by train to Grimsby for the minesweepers. Going round the village in those days was not what it would be today. There were houses on three sides of the green, one little row of cottages on the green in front of the Old Manor was called Dormer Row. They were built by an old lady who lived at Evenley Hall. She wasn't going to have people gossiping at their doors as she drove by, therefore there were no front doors until quite recently. There were magnificent great elm trees on the Green—I think six or seven of them—and a road went across from the Old Manor corner to the pub. In spite of these obstacles cricket was played there. Sadly, the time came when the elms had to be lopped and then the Dutch Elm disease finished them off. A farmer called Joe Martin carried pails of milk across the Green from the farm to his house next to the Old Manor on a yoke—a sort of wooden bar across his shoulders with a bucket dangling at each end.

Euan should have gone to Harrow, where his father had been and was Head of the school, but at that time I had evacuees living with us who came from Harrow to get away from the flying bombs and as Malvern School was all mixed in with Harrow I didn't think it was a good idea for

Euan to go there. Now I think I was wrong and I know Euan regretted very much that he didn't go. He went to a good Quaker School called Leighton Park.

Those evacuees from Harrow, Gus and Oliver Sherret, are still in touch with me. After the war they built a house and called it 'Evenley'. Twice more, as they built larger homes, they still called them 'Evenley' in memory of their happy time here!

When Steve and Euan were home for the Easter holidays from their prep school one cold and miserable night I asked them to make a good fire. They did, they set fire to the chimney! I heard the awful WHOOF of it The boys were keen I should send for the fire brigade. When they arrived it was the NFS - not experienced - and they had a handbook with them which they read! Their ladders were not long enough to start from the top so they came into the house and squirted water up the chimney putting sandbags round the fireplace to protect the carpets. Euan made tea for the men and it became quite a party before they reluctantly returned to Brackley!

Steve, in uniform, Euan, Rosemary & Sue

On another occasion in a hard frost the boys wrapped straw around a pipe and set fire to it to thaw it! Those old pipes were made of cast iron.

I am going to break off from Evenley to tell you about a Great Great Aunt of yours called Katherine Marshall, my mother's sister, who was a rabid suffragette. She was one of Mrs. Pankhurst's "right hand women" and went to prison. As children Wuppy and I were thrilled by all the stories she used to tell us. Last week, March 1993, there was an account in the Daily Telegraph about some ceremony held at Mrs. Pankhurst's statue in Victoria Embankment gardens. Aunt Kitty was responsible for that statue being there. I well remember her going off to see the Prime Minister, Stanley Baldwin, in her best clothes. She badgered him until she got her way. She was also mentioned not long ago because she threw a cricket ball through a Cabinet Minister's window and it is mentioned in Wisden's Book of Cricket Memorabilia!

Now back to Evenley. The dear old house always coped with any occasion. The first was when Patsy was married and the reception was in the house. When Steve was 21 I gave a party for the village and engaged entertainers from Oxford who staged a show in the Working Men's Club room, which is now our excellent village shop. We had a houseful of relations staying for it and it was a tremendous success. You can imagine in the days before television there was nothing much in the way of entertainment!

Then came my mother's funeral. It was a family party - my mother loved parties and for people to enjoy themselves. Then I think it must have been Steve's wedding to Margret who came from Canada. Her parents were dead so the wedding was here. Then there was Caroline's christening in 1960, Sue's wedding in 1963 followed by Andrew's christening.

The house must have been stretched to its limits in 1960, the year you all came to live with me after you had been in Australia and your father's army career came to an end. He had to find a job, then a home. Caroline was born in the Cottage Hospital in Brackley. You and David had Hazel, your dear Nan, to look after you and you both went to a pre-prep day school in Brackley. There was a time when I remember you going to the village school. Later on when you and David went to Stowe you used to come out for meals and I was lucky because I could go to your school speech days and see David in school plays - he was a wonderful actor as well as being Captain of Rugger and Cricket and Head Boy. You climbed the roofs of that great house. I also remember coming to collect you at the end of term and seeing a great quantity of desks and chairs on

14

the lawn on the north front - I'm afraid you had a hand in that and also with a Mini car sitting in the middle of a cricket pitch! You used to ring church bells.

Then Caroline came to Tudor Hall near Banbury and I used to fetch her and her friends to spend Sundays with me. Later on Nick came to school at Beachborough, Westbury, so again I was able to be included in seeing the excellent school plays and going to lovely carol services. Nick used to bring his friends out for meals. His special friend, Toby, curiously turned out to be the grandson of my friend Joan Hobson who brought the pies I have already told you about. It was always a relief when I got Toby back to school without any mishaps - he was a harum scarum boy! Nick became Head Boy.

My other grandchildren used to come and stay whilst their parents had a holiday so the old house and Evenley were well known to them all.

Sue, from an early age, always had a pony. The first one was called Conker, a lovely, lively little creature. Gradually the size of the ponies grew as Sue grew, ending up with the splendid horse Cheerful which she hunted. There was always life in the stables. There were also several sad occasions when my dogs and the cats were buried in the orchard with bitter tears and the help of my good neighbour Kitty Fox.

Sue & her Pony

Some time after the war a new house was built in the village and I became very upset as more and more houses sprang up. I was on the Parish

Council and knew we had little power to control what sort of buildings were put up and I used to think I'd have to leave the village. I couldn't bear it. The faster the houses went up the more the character of the village changed. Cars began to appear round the green as there were no garages and that horrid word "commuter" came into being. Cottages that went for £100 when the Evenley Hall Estate was sold, (I bought one cottage for £80 - I went down to the house agent in Brackley and said "I don't mind giving you £80 for that cottage") were fetching thousands of pounds. In time the village was put on the mains and we had to install bathrooms and proper sinks into the cottages. I remember when the row of cottages up Bone Hill used the bank opposite their cottages for making fires and boiling their clothes and cooking on them. I don't know why they chose to do this as there was a common boiler in "a hovel" for the use of the cottages. There was a deep well for their water.

Just to show you how different the traffic was in those days, Sue was able to ride along the main road to Brackley - rather a different road from the A43 of today. There was a special sort of cheese she liked and she rode into town to get it. By the time she arrived home there wasn't much cheese left! She went to a very good little school near the Town Hall which she hated. At one time I found a loose box in Brackley so that she could ride in and leave her pony and then ride home again. One day she rode an enormous horse called Shortie belonging to a neighbour to the blacksmith in the town to be shod. After school she collected him and was leading him out when a friend of mine saw her and offered to give her a leg up. Sue said she could manage and went to the Town Hall where she climbed onto a window sill and from there into the saddle. She was about 8 years old at that time.

Once upon a time it was said "an Englishman's word was his bond" and, just to show you what it was like when honesty was the norm, I was in London and went to the Army and Navy stores to buy a fox fur - all the fashion then, head one end bush the other - and was asked where it was to be sent. I said I really wanted to wear it then and there. I was asked for my telephone number, it was checked against the telephone directory and, having written a cheque, I was allowed to take it Bank cards were many years off at that time.

In those days one never locked doors or windows. The bantams used to come in through the downstairs kitchen window and one time they ate the centre of a precious scone I had made! I had bantams for many years, their delicious little eggs were a great help in the war. They were good company, but very bad gardeners - they scratched up things that were newly planted. One old cock lived for many years. I'm afraid we also ate them -though not me as they were my friends!

There was a good train service to London from the Top Station. My mother and Wuppy could go to London for the day for 10s. each, 7s.6d. for the railway ticket and 2s.6d. For lunch. They had a taxi to go to the station, but walked home (about two miles).

Once King George VI, the Queen and Princesses came by train to Brackley and from there they went to Silverstone by road for the motor racing. I went down Mill Lane to see the Royal train and hopefully a Royal face, but when the train came lumbering along the single line track all the windows were steamed up! When it arrived at the Bottom Station which had been re-painted for the occasion and the Mayor and his party all there to receive them, it was found that the drop from the Royal coach to the platform was too deep - some old kipper boxes had to be brought to make a step!

A charming photograph of Her Majesty the Queen looking truly regal in a powder blue two-piece, as she turns to acknowledge the cheers of the crowd at Brackley Station.

The King & Queen arriving at Brackley from Banbury Guardian 1950

In May 1949 there was the Grand Prix at Silverstone and I heard that the

Crown Hotel in Brackley was offering £1 a head per night for anyone who would provide bed and breakfast. £1, that was a lot of money. Being always short of money I rang up and said I would have two or three people to stay. The Manager seemed a bit surprised that I should offer to have guests. I said it would be all right if he would vet those he sent. He did ring up and just said two people would come and that was all. It was getting dark when I found in the porch that the two people were dusky Italians. One was the manager of the Italian team, and the other was the brother of the winner of the previous year - Villoresi. The manager went straight to bed and the house resounded to his terrific snores. The other went off to Silverstone to prepare his brother's car. I gave them breakfast in the old kitchen and I remember they liked the flowers on the table. They were to come back for a second night - that meant £4 for me! However, the manager rang up to say they would not be returning as they had been ordered to go straight to the coast, but that I would be paid the same amount. In my visitor's book I see Villoresi wrote "With much thank. I remember".

Once a nephew, Spencer Bell, came on leave when he was doing his National Service. I asked him what he wanted to do and he said he'd like to see the Silverstone circuit so off we went. When we arrived there was no-one about so we drove round the circuit in XS 4636 (the old car already mentioned in these memoirs)! I think we went the wrong way round and wondered what would happen if we met a race coming the other way! As we drove away I did see all the notices along the road saying "Keep Out".

In 1951 for Silverstone I put up an Australian sheep farmer called Frank Lobb who brought Wing Commander G. Cummings who flew the first Canberra to Australia (with four overnight stops) and also a Test Pilot. They must have found the bathroom very primitive. The first thing they wanted to do was have a wash. I expect a shower would have been more in their line. Frank Lobb came back again the following year and brought his mother. Later on he came once more and brought his fiancé. I think the Old Manor must have exerted its charm which overcame any of its shortcomings. I wonder what they paid. There was not even a second loo in the house until your father had the good idea of going through the wall by the kitchen, which I had moved upstairs, and then a little cloakroom was built.

Perhaps I should tell you about Canons Ashby which is now National Trust and open to visitors. It was a wonderful old house and had a beautiful garden There were three Miss Drydens and their brother. We called them Cousin Mary, Cousin Clara, and one who had married called Louise was incredibly ugly and we called her Big Bear. The house was so lovely. When Queen Mary went to visit it she overstayed her time by 3/4 of an hour she was so fascinated with it and some lovely embroidery. I remember taking Euan there as a little boy and he was entranced because the horse that pulled the mowing machine was wearing boots. One of my aunts, Aunt Celia, who was my mother's other sister, went to stay there. She was a bit psychic and thought the house was haunted. She went to the local post office and sent herself a telegram to say she was to go home at once. You will have to look at the family tree to see what the connection was, but I know my grandfather was first cousin to the Drydens of his generation.

Just to round off the people who took refuge in the Old Manor during the War - there was Muriel, your Great Aunt, who was a dispatch rider. She worked in London and used to go to No. 10 Downing Street. She came to me for any bit of leave she had. People in the train would ask her where she wanted to get out and then she went to sleep until someone woke her at her station. One night I found she had bolted the door of the little bedroom. When I asked her why she said she was fed up with the Vicar and the Blanchflowers. By that time the Vicar had a bed in the dining room - I can't think how long that lasted! His wife had gone to stay elsewhere, and then he left and every weekend for months I put up a Vicar who came from Oxford during the interregnum.

Muriel sent her daughter to Canada for the war, but Thyrza came back just towards the end of it. The flying bombs started and as Muriel was living near London Thyrza was sent to Evenley. She knew nothing about rationing and wanted to eat marmalade with her bacon - both very strictly rationed!

My cousin Margaret White was living in Burma when war broke out. Her husband was called up as he was in the Naval Reserve. He and her

19

father were against Margaret and her daughter Nona taking the risk of travelling home. Sadly, when she did come back her husband had deserted her after the long separation (though they afterwards married again) and her mother and father had died. I felt I must be at Southampton to meet her. Petrol was very tight at that time, but the man who lived where Kitty Fox lived had a bit extra because he was a poultry farmer and let me have some which I carried over the field from his house. In those days there were no signposts. They were all taken down in case of a German invasion. I set off to stay with dear friends near Salisbury for the night to be near Southampton. When I arrived I said I'd better check what time the boat was due the next day only to be told it had already berthed and everyone had gone There had been strikes at some ports so the ship arrived early. I just had tea with my friends and turned tail and went back to Evenley feeling I had utterly failed my cousins. They arrived in Evenley and stayed until they were organised. I remember having to devise an extra bedroom by putting a bed at the foot of the attic stairs with a chair and screen!

The history of Evenley would not be complete without remembering Mrs. Steggles "Mrs. Steggie", my invaluable 'daily' who for over 30 years kept the Old Manor in good order, who helped when grandchildren came and when we went on expeditions to Woburn, to see the birds at Bourton-on-the-Water and for picnics. When you wrote to me from Australia or wherever you got to you always sent your love to Mrs. Steggie. She and I had only one little tiff - she was not well and I said she should go to the doctor. She replied I should give her the credit of knowing when she needed to go to the doctor! I felt rebuked.

The only time she was not allowed to come to my aid was when Rosemary, who had had a form of meningitis, came home from hospital in Oxford unable to walk. I fetched her, feeling ill myself, and that night found I had a bad go of German measles. No-one dare come near us because it was the time of a polio epidemic and there was the fear of infection.

Rosemary was married in London at St. Michael's Chester Square in December 1951. The war ended in 1945, but there was still a great shortage of things. For instance there was only white china to be had and we had difficulty getting clothes for Rosemary's trousseau. I do not remember if there were still clothes coupons.

The next transition the Old Manor went through was when Wuppy came to live with me after Uncle Stephen's death in 1976. We made the old kitchen into her sitting room where she had her own possessions and very charming it was. She was always so clever at arranging her bits and pieces. She went back to her own bedroom which was hers before she was married. She was received back into the village with open arms and called "Miss Mace"! She had spent her married life or nearly 40 years in Norfolk and was rather cut off from all my family and was happy to be amongst you all again.

Sadly, she was very frail for the five years we had together. We began to realise the Old Manor and the garden was too much for us to cope with. We wandered around the village wondering where we could make a home, but there was nowhere to go. Then in July 1982 she died. We had a beautiful funeral service in Evenley then Sue took me to her old village, Great Fransham, where she was buried. I gave new churchyard gates to Evenley in her memory. These Eric kindly designed. They were made by Malcolm Pipes in Carlton Hursthwaite.

Wuppy, Cicely and Teasel

Wuppy had shared the expenses of the Old Manor with me. Now I was

21

faced with the necessity to do something with myself. There was only one answer and that was to build. What a shock it was to the family to think of me leaving the old house! However, everyone came round to the idea and were very stalwart in supporting me.

The first difficulty was to get planning permission to build in my field. There were headlines in the local papers...... "SHOULD PLANNERS BEND THEIR RULES TO HELP AN OLD LADY?" I didn't mind it being said that I was over 80, but I was furious at being called an old lady! There were stormy meetings of the planning people and then the headline SOUTH NORTHANTS DISTRICT COUNCIL PLANNERS LET HEART COME BEFORE POLICY DESPITE 'REMEMBER RULES' CALL" and by one vote I was given permission.

A friend who had made a home for herself nearby told me she knew the architect, Eric Throssell. I rang him up and for the first time in my life was faced with talking to an answering machine! I can remember him coming for the first time in September 1983 and he loved the Old Manor so that was a good beginning.

Now came a time of great excitement and interest as Eric began to draw up the plans - and re-draw them - and take such infinite care over every detail. On the 5th March 1984 the building began. It was a wonderful summer that year and we often had tea in the garden discussing the details. The builders were never held up by bad weather. When the house was nearing completion Eric's artist friend Jean Webster came and helped with her excellent advice to choose the colours for the walls and September 11th was moving day! I could never have been ready for it without Sue's great help and hard work.

Sue and Eric both came to help and Caroline was there too, busy changing electric light plugs. The furniture all fitted in well because Eric had made just the right house for it. There are lovely wood floors as I was not having fitted carpets and the charming hall and staircase which I had specially asked for. I remember when everyone had gone on the night of the 11th just sitting feeling quite overcome because I had such a lovely home. Many were the housewarming parties and visitors who came and were all full of admiration and praise of Manor Cottage.

The other little thing I must tell you is that the village thought it was extraordinary because I'd had a new house built and brought along my old bath! That old bath is a true Victorian and I wouldn't be without it!

There was still much to do because the garden didn't exist. The house sat in a field, amidst rubble and chickweed. Then my new neighbour Janet Cropley, who is a landscape gardener, came to the rescue and with her help it began to take shape

There was also the Old Manor to be sold. The house agents were very fed up because I kept saying I would not sell to the people they brought to see the house. Then mercifully the Bentleys came. They love the old house and once again it is the home of young people and I have been fortunate to have them as my neighbours. On a lovely sunny day at the end of June 1991 they very kindly had a wonderful party in their garden for friends from the village to celebrate my 90th birthday. Many of my family came including my sister-in-law, Jean Donaldson, and her daughter who travelled down from Scotland especially for the occasion. The week before, you will remember, we were all with Sue for a real family reunion. Unfortunately, the weather did its worst! None the less it was a very special and memorable day.

Two other parties must be mentioned. There was a time when Euan and Jenny lived in a spectacular house called Pednor and I was asked to go for a night during the summer holidays of 1971 to see the family. I suggested to Sue I might have a cup of coffee with her on my way there. She said they were going out to lunch. Instead I would go on my way home. When I arrived, dressed in a fairly old cotton frock, and gardening shoes, with my bath towel over my arm, all ready to work, Euan and Jenny greeted me in very tidy clothes, saying they hadn't really done anything about my 70th birthday. They then opened the drawing room door and the first person I saw was Sue with six months old Nick on her knee. I looked beyond her and gradually it dawned on me my whole family was there, all in their best clothes! What a wonderful surprise. Jenny had prepared a lavish feast for us. I always thought it must have been such fun for all of you. You and Diana were sixteen, the eldest of my grandchildren, and were part of the conspiracy of this secret plan. All the cars were hidden away in other people's drives. Steve had flown his family up from Hurn to a private landing strip not far away. You were all gathered together waiting for my arrival - and I had jolly nearly gone into an antique shop on my way!

On another occasion, in the summer of 1989, I was invited by my neighbour, Janet Cropley, to go up for a drink. It was rather a long invitation, which made me wonder if it was a birthday party or something special. I was assured they were only having an old friend. When I arrived in their lovely garden I found a large party of friends from the village. Sue and John were invited, they drove down to Brackley not to risk being seen passing my home. Janet led me to a table upon which was an iced cake. Instead of the usual birthday message it said it was for me on the 50th year of my living in Evenley. What a wonderfully kind idea and all provided for by generous friends. It was a very happy occasion. I think the element of surprise is great fun.

It was Janet's idea to plant a tree to commemorate my 90th birthday. Such was the generosity of friends that many trees were planted, all the hard work done by Janet and Bob.

Once, when Steve used to fly, we both happened to hear on the wireless that some illegal immigrants had landed on the old airfield at Finmere, five miles away. We had the same thought - if they could, why not Steve? Sure enough he did bring a friend up for tea one day. He flew over the house and I knew it was time to go and collect them.

Though, Stephen, of course you know all about it I think the story of Sarah Wynn must be included. She was an ancestor and there was a portrait of her painted by Hopner. At the end of the last century for some unknown reason this portrait was missing. My grandfather wrote in a

Manor Cottage

24

book that was published in 1904 that he hoped it might be found. In May, 1988 you, Stephen, being familiar with the picture because of prints and an engraving of it, went to a sale room in Kirby Lonsdale the day before the auction and looked through some pictures stacked against a wall and there you found it. I well remember your excitement when you rang up to check a few details to be sure it really was the missing picture. She now hangs on the staircase at Manor Cottage for my lifetime though she belongs to you. She is beautiful. She was the girlfriend of the Duke of Clarence, but because she was not of Royal blood he could not marry her and he was sent off by George IV in a frigate to the East Indies. What an amazing chance that she is back in the family.

Sarah Wynn painted by Hopner

Well there it is Stephen, a fragment that may give you a glimpse "through all the changing scenes of life".
  With my love to you and all my grandchildren.

  Your devoted grandmother,

  Omi

N.B. It is entirely due to my friend Jessica Church who lives down my lane that these memoirs have been written - she not only supplied the books for me to scribble in, the encouragement and interest that kept me going, but also did all the typing. I am most grateful to her.
April 1993

Cicely after her special service for her 95th birthday 23rd June1996

LIFE

WAS LIKE

THAT

Growing up in Evenley

by

WILLIAM BUGGINS

Bill Buggins and his wife Mattie

This history or chronicle of events is the work of a countryman who has lived and worked the whole of his life in agriculture at Evenley.

It describes the progress and events in Evenley from 1900 until after the Second World War, showing the changes taking place during this period of time.

I am grateful to several inhabitants of Evenley for help given me in this work - to Mr. Norman Grierson, who drew the cover; Mrs. Elizabeth Caley and Miss Ann Caley, who typed the final draft; and Mr. Richard Bright, who saw the book through the press.

It is dedicated to Evenley Parish Council, some of its members having asked me and prompted me to write this history in the first instance.

Any profits are being given to the Cancer Research Campaign.

W.G. (Bill) Buggins

June 1976

LIFE WAS LIKE THAT

I have a good memory, even today in my seventies. I am now in retirement and the reason I am writing this is to show what changes have taken place since 1900 in Evenley parish. Comparing the time of which I write to the present day, what changes there have been. From travel on foot, horse and train to travel to the moon. Surely, no generation has been in such a position before to witness so much change in such a short time. As for the good old days and "You never had it so good", I will leave it at that and let someone else decide. Everyone can have their own opinion, right or wrong. I have mine.

The changes, the comings and goings at Evenley and the progress it has made - yes I have watched my own house rise from a rental of two shillings a week to four pounds a week, and many other cottages from a rental of two shillings to three or four pounds a week, looking the same as they were then, apart from some alteration inside. Evenley's water supply has changed to sewage and sanitation; candles and paraffin to electric lighting. Its transport, its agriculture and machinery, its horseflesh and the railways have changed. The Men's Club is the village shop. The Green, the Church and other properties have changed. Its beech trees, its parklands, its wild birds and flowers....I'll go back again and see, if I can, how all this change for better or worse has come about. I have been blessed with a good wife and mother who has shared my grief and joy and also fairly good health. Now I have time to spare to write this. I have much to be thankful for.

An Early Memory

My recollections began at an early age, around three years, with fire. I learned afterwards from my father and mother that it had been a very hot and dry summer and harvest was in progress that year. There was a field known as Mill Way that had been planted with beans and the beans had been shed loose on the ground in great profusion by the heat of the sun. So there we were, 'leasing' or gleaning beans off the ground, several families fathers and mothers together with the children—night after night, all picking up beans.

One night, the sun had just gone down in a great ball of fire, when someone said, "Look thonder—fire"!! and my father threw down his bucket and ran with several other men towards the scene of the fire. The sky was red and huge billows of smoke appeared to be coming towards us - a scene, I remember quite well to this day and am never likely to forget. The Pump Farm at Cottisford was on fire and this had in turn spread to a corn field and into a covert, a young plantation of well established larch trees of approximately thirty acres and it scared us all so much.

Mother said there was pandemonium with all the kids bawling when we were left to walk home alone. Whether it was Dad running away or the glow of the fire that scared us, no one can say. Strange to say, it stopped the gleaning and we did not go any more after that.

The covert was named to this day as the Burnt Covert. I learned in later years that the fire was caused by a bottle lying under a haystack.

Road across the Green

EVENLEY - THE VILLAGE AND HALL

Few records seem to exist to show what Evenley looked like before 1865, but what has been handed down by mouth from one generation to another by men who could neither read nor write.

It appears that Evenley comprised a lot of thatched cottages to serve the farms of that time and that most of them became dangerous and unfit to live in. There was a line of cottages from near the Church to the Manor House, continuing on towards Lower Farm; now Evenley Hall Farm. There was another line running from the School corner down to the Manor House like an inverted L. There were not houses on the eastern side of the village and only two or three on the southern side.

Evenley Hall Farm

It is said that it was Mr. Sidney Pierrepoint who planned the village as it is today. Most of the thatched cottages were pulled down in this family's time at Evenley and most of its cottages were rebuilt and the Green laid out like it is today and having a road made across the Green from the Manor House to the Red Lion to give easy access out of the village for horse drawn vehicles. The road was taken up and closed by the County Council and was grassed over, making a big improvement to the Green for football and cricket and providing a larger area for children to play in safety from motor and other traffic.

There was a school and this was also a thatched building and a new one built in its place bears the date 1834. Very little was learned in the old school. Many boys did not attend school at all, and when they were ten years of age were in regular work on the farms where their fathers were employed.

The School became redundant in 1966 and all the village children were sent to Brackley for their schooling. The owners of the School and the Village Green having left Evenley, this property was acquired by the Parish Council and the School was to become Evenley Village Hall. The Men's Clubroom, that had acted as the Village Hall so well since 1925, was sold and became the Village Shop and Post Office.

The Village Stocks stood at the north east end of the village near an elm tree. The stocks were taken down and burned when the Green was laid out about 1850. The tree is still standing today, being known as the Stocks Tree. There were nine elm trees on the Green from 1905 to 1917. The Stocks Tree had the top blown off and was a hollow stump in my young days. The top has grown again, having grown to its present state in sixty odd years, but the tree suffered fresh damage in a gale in 1976. There are four of the nine trees left standing on the Green today.

The Stocks

There was, too, the Pound standing at the fork of the roads to Mixbury and Finmere. This was a walled-in yard and had a pig-sty and a small lockup barn for the locking up for the night of a horse or pony, sheep, pigs, dogs or other animals that had strayed until their owners came along to claim them.

Mr. Sidney Pierrepont, who was a Civil Engineer, made Evenley Ponds by damming its streams, the Fish Pond, the New Pond and Four Corners Pond to provide water in case of fire. He planned the making-up of the roadway near the gas works over the Ouse going into Brackley. This place was in full flood in the winter time and made a journey in and out of Brackley a hazardous operation and the same on the Oxford road at Ladybridge, on the Mixbury road at Fishpool and the road to Finmere near the spring.

The meadow land from Brackley gas works to Evenley Mill, it is said, was always flooded and more or less useless until he had a dyke known as the Carrier dug out and sluices made to control the water of the Ouse basin in Evenley parish. It is now good pasture land.

Evenley Hall Estate

Evenley Hall

35

Francis Bassett built Evenley Hall in the 18th Century. It then came into the possession of the Pierrepoint family. They did not farm the land that belonged to the estate. It was all leased to a Thomas Andrews who farmed its three farms for a great number of years.

It was around 1845 to 1850 that my father's family settled in Evenley. After the Pierrepoint family came the Campbell family, about 1876. This family lived at the Hall for twelve years. It was then occupied by Major W.H Allen's father and mother in 1889. In 1897 the Hall caught fire and was almost destroyed. It was rebuilt and another wing added and so remains today.

The parkland around the Hall was well wooded and carried a large number of oak, elm, beech and chestnut trees and many had their branches tied with strong iron bands and chains. Today there are none of these trees standing on the eastern and southern faces of Evenley Hall. The Front Park remains today as it was in the years 1900 to 1914. The Mill Farm was added to the estate in 1912.

Evenley Hall had a deep artesian well and this was kept full with a second supply of water from the reservoir at Stockwell and was driven to the Hall by two rams until the New Pond was made. A thatched wheelhouse was built below the New Pond at Stockwell and this housed a large water wheel about thirty feet in diameter. It was driven by the water from the New Pond that filled its buckets to make it revolve. A new spring was tapped and pumps were installed and a new pipeline laid to Evenley Hall that gave it a new supply. The rams could be heard working when I was a boy, but as the years went by, they fell into disuse and ceased to function. In 1912, a wind pump was erected to give further help to pump water at Stockwell. In 1924, a petrol engine was installed and these were in use for a long period until electricity was installed at Evenley in 1934. Water was also laid to several drinking troughs in the parklands round Evenley Hall for watering its livestock.

The park and pasture lands on the eastern and southern sides of Evenley Hall, having been detached as part of that estate, were separated from the Front Park and Evenley Hall in 1939. These acres carried a large number of fine old ash and elm trees that had been protected and kept together with massive iron chains. A great wave of tree felling took place at this time and all the elm trees were cut down and burned to make charcoal. Perhaps some of this charcoal was used in the defence of the Country by being turned into gunpowder. I do not know.

It seems such a crime and waste to see these fine old elms in a funeral pyre of fire and smoke. Most had a girth at their trunks five feet in diameter and were perhaps three or four hundred years old. They were homes of the woodpecker and jackdaw and often as a boy I had seen the red squirrel running from tree to tree.

The Manor House

The Manor House in snow

This was perhaps Evenley's oldest house. During the 1900's it was a bakery where most of the bread for Evenley was made and baked. Mothers of that time put ingredients of lard, sugar and currants in a baking tin, mostly on Saturdays and when the ovens would be cooling after Saturday's bread was baked, the baker would, for no charge at all, mix in the dough and there was a large dough cake ready for tea about four o'clock.

There are also near the Manor House two old thatched cottages that look much the same as they were long ago. These belonged to the Manor House at this time.

The Rectory Farmhouse

This is another old house and has several old buildings and was farmed for many years by the Hopcraft family. With Plomers Firs, Barley Mow, Astwick Farm and White House Farm it formed part of the Manor of Evenley, of which the patron is Magdalen College, Oxford. These farms were all sold separately in 1922 and 1923 and are now all privately owned, some having changed ownership since these years. There are very few old trees standing on these farmlands today.

The Land

There were many acres of land in the direction of Juniper and Cottisford that were uncultivated and were known as heathlands that formed a large plain that grew a lot of gorse and thorn bushes. This was controlled by fire and was grazed by the livestock of several farmers, horses, cattle and sheep all branded and running together. There were many young piglets and lambs farrowed and lambed under these conditions and there were many disputes as to their ownership.

The Evenley Enclosure

The Enclosure Act of 1778 altered all this. Ditches were dug out and a thorn fence was planted on one side of the ditch and the parcels, plots and fields were measured out in acres and decimal points of acres and are marked out on ordnance maps the same as today. There are three parcels or areas of land known today as Plomers Firs, or Plowman's Furze Heath, Cottisford Heath and Juniper Heath. Juniper Heath was a favourite place for tramps and gipsies and one time was their camping ground and was the scene of many fights with fisticuffs. After the Enclosure Act, things became more settled and farming was better in every way.

THE WAY WE LIVED

Most parishes were alike and run in the same way. Each village was schooled and carried on in exactly the same manner as at Evenley, I speak also for its neighbouring villages and its people, more or less, all coming under their own parish and councils respectively, just as they are today. They were like large families. Men, women and children were as clean and contented as those times would allow and were very neighbourly and respectful to one another. There were inevitable comings and goings, but the work and play went on with the people happy on the whole, quite as well as the people of today, with their motor cars, TV sets and other pleasures.

The Shop

There was a shop at Evenley, chiefly for sweets and tobacco. Groceries

39

in the main were ordered and had to be picked up and carried away, walking across the Park from Brackley. There was also the local Evenley carrier who would load them from Buckingham and Banbury and deliver them from his horse and van.

If anything of consequence was purchased, it was mainly from the shops in Brackley and carried by hand on the footpath across Evenley Park. Most of the villages around Brackley were in the same way. There were pony and traps going into Brackley and sometimes one could get a lift in this way. It was all right when it was fine, but a different matter when it was raining or snowing and sometimes had to be put off and manage as well as could be until Monday to make the trip. Evenley Park was well trodden in those days.

Pony & Trap

The Price of Things

Food, drink and tobacco were very cheap during these days, 1900 - 1914. Some things fluctuated as they became scarce. Eggs would be two for three halfpence when plentiful, three pence each when scarce. Bread kept a reasonable price—three pence to four pence a loaf. Good meat, beef, pork and lamb was sixpence a pound. Most mothers were able to buy their meat and have good, meaty marrow bones given in with their joints for making puddings, pies and soups. The bones were not cut like they are today and were a lot bigger, due to the animals being bigger and fatter in those days. The wild rabbit was cheap and plentiful and made many dinners of puddings and pies.

Oranges were perhaps the only foreign fruit of the time and they came in just before Christmas and finished shortly before Easter. They could be bought at forty for a shilling and so a lot of marmalade was made by the mothers, who were very skilful at jam and wine making. Apples, blackberries, damsons, plums, marrows, rhubarb were turned into jam in most households, to come out in the winter time and eke out the food supply. Wine making was practised too. Parsnip, elderberry, dandelion, rhubarb, sloe and others were made in great profusion.

Beer was strong in these years, two to three pence a pint. Whisky was three and six a bottle, rum and gin three shillings a bottle. Many inns and public houses would serve a pint of beer, bread, cheese and pickles and a penny packet of Woodbines for three pence for a quick lunch in these years. Tobacco was cheap, cut and plug shag being smoked by most pipe smokers and there were a lot of smokers who liked their old black and browned clay pipes. Players cigarettes, Wills Gold Flake were three pence for a packet of ten. These cigarettes had a picture card packed inside and a boy would run to the shop or pub to buy a packet of cigarettes for the older men to get the fag-card. Many boys collected whole sets of these cards and a lot of swapping was done for them at this time.

Telling the Time

Clocks and watches were kept to the right time by the sounding of a steam hooter on the roof of Brackley Brewery, every day except Sunday at one o'clock and this could be heard quite plainly at Evenley.

There was Evenley Church clock in good working order, chiming the quarter hours and striking the hours, Evenley Hall clock and the school clock.

The Newspapers

There were daily papers at Evenley, but scarce and few in number. The daily papers came by the postman and only a few could afford to take one in daily. There was, however, a Sunday newspaper that was brought in from Brackley and delivered at the homes of the folk and so most people were able to read a newspaper on Sundays.   News of any importance was rather late in reaching the folk.

Mr. Shelford, who became Schoolmaster in 1875, used to inform us in school from his Daily Mail of anything important and after his dinner would take the paper out to the school corner and read it to several pensioners gathered there when it was fine.

There was one topic of news talked about a lot and that was the county cricket scores and the exploits of W.G. Grace, M.A. Noble, Victor Trumper and others of that time.   Then there were the football results and the Russo-Japanese War which followed in 1905 and was talked about a lot.   There was the Sydney Street Siege of Peter the Painter and I well remember how the Titanic sailed in 1912 on her maiden voyage from Queenstown, read out to the school by Mr. Shelford and how two days later he came into school and told us that the Titanic had struck an iceberg and sunk with great loss of life.

There were other events of those times told in school: Bleriot had flown across the Channel by aeroplane;   wireless had led to the arrest of Dr. Crippen and other stories.   News travelled slowly in those days.

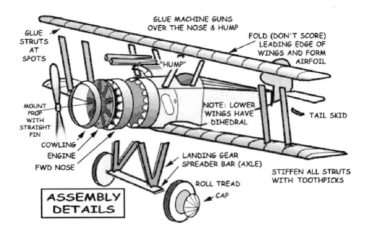

The Sopwith Camel

My grandmother took in a picture paper for my grandfather.   He liked to see the pictures and he could neither read nor write. But he could draw a horse from memory, as good as any artist, for he loved his horses and so, if he wanted to know something about a picture that he had seen, my grandmother, who was able to read and write well, would tell him all about it. She was also the doctor's right hand at Evenley. She was, as every village had, the village nurse and midwife. Perhaps she will come into the story again.

Welfare

Most villages and places had their own sick benefit clubs and societies to provide help when the people could not work through illness and to pay the doctors' and other fees. The National Health Service had not come into being. Evenley had such a club. A subscription, though small, was paid by most of the labouring menfolk and was of great help to provide sickness benefits.

There were two doctors who lived in Brackley at this time, each having his own surgery and they made their rounds weekly for those who were too ill to travel into Brackley. During the early years of 1900 to 1910, the doctors had their own transport by pony and trap and bicycle and were driven by their own grooms or coachmen. Later, they had their own cars and were chauffeur driven.

Most villages had a doctor's help-nurse-midwife, a woman who would attend those who needed help until the doctor arrived. My grandmother, Sarah George, was this for many years at Evenley and gave her services freely to those in need. She attended at the 'first and last' for a great many parishioners of Evenley. Most childbirths were in their own homes. There were no maternity homes, as is the case today. The aged and infirm were looked after by their own children and by the neighbours living nearby. There were some who had no children and then the cry was heard, "Don't take me to the workhouse! I don't want to die in the workhouse"!! But there was nowhere else for these poor unfortunates and so they are taken away to be looked after as well as it was possible in those days and years.

Until 1908 there were no pensions. It was Public Assistance - Poor Law Relief was administered by the Board of Guardians. The sum of two shillings and sixpence and three shillings, rising later to five shillings was paid. This was their pension and in those days barely enough to live on. There were some aged people who were too proud and would not accept it and it was frowned upon to take Parish Relief. How some of these people existed at all was always a mystery. There were, too, the Oddfellows and Foresters Societies at Brackley, also Brackley Accidental Society Benefit Clubs.

The Cottage Pig

Although the hours were long and the work heavy and tough, men and boys went walking to work, cheerful and happy and contented with their lot for such low wages. They still found time for recreation and to attend to their families' needs, working their gardens and allotments.

Most cottages had a pigsty attached to their outhouses and most of the pigsties were occupied by a pig, to be killed and cured into bacon, with a taste and smell the like of which is unobtainable today. The piglets were bought in the spring by the cottagers. They were fed twice a day for the start on scraps left over from the families' homes and waste from the gardens - greenstuff and anything suitable for pigs to eat, gathered by all the family, mothers playing their part in this. The feeding and rearing were carried on throughout the summer months, with father doing the cleaning out of the pigsty. After a short time toppings were added to the pig feed and the pig grew up as one of the family. As the pig grew, more was given him to eat to keep him contented. When September arrived, the pig was given a further addition to his feed by adding barley meal and boiled potatoes and this went on to the end of November and December.

It was now time for the pig killing. The butcher came from Brackley to do this job and the pigs were despatched, first by stunning. Many tears were shed at this time by the younger members of the family and mother wiped her eyes. But it was soon forgotten. The pig was cut up the next day. The head and feet of the pig and other parts were used up first, while the sides and hams were put in a salting, in pickle with salt for three weeks. After this the sides or flitches were taken out of the brine and they were wrapped in cloth and were hung on the walls of the cottage to dry. What pictures they made! Two hams and two sides of bacon. Some families killed and cured two pigs a year. Most pigs killed weighed from twelve to twenty score deadweight. There were backbone pies, brawn, hog pudding, chitterlings, home cured lard, faggots and other delicacies in profusion, shared with friends and family, neighbours and pensioners.

A pig club ran for a good many years at Evenley. The members paid a sum of money per pig, about half a crown, to be insured against loss or sickness for a year.

Evenley Feast Day

If the Feast of St. George, patron saint of St. George's Church, Evenley fell on a Sunday, there was no celebration held that day, but it was held on the next day, Monday. The showmen came to the Green after midnight on Sunday and early in the morning proceeded to set up their swingboats and roundabouts and other sideshows ready for the evening. There would be a cricket match in the afternoon for the men, married and single and the violinists of Evenley came out to play for a dance in the evening for all to take part in.

Club Feast Day

Club Day

It was holiday of the Club and village also on Club Day. This was usually held on a certain day in the month of July every year. The

45

members and parishioners would meet together on the Green and with a band march to Church for their Service of Thanksgiving by the Vicar of Evenley, the Rev. Edward Worsley, who served the village from 1871 to 1923. The bells were rung and the band played for the hymns as well as the organ. Returning from Church, the Club sat down to dinner and this was held at the Malthouse Barn, this having been cleaned out for the occasion. This barn today is the village shop and post office and was formerly, about 1925, adapted and known as the Evenley Men's Club.

There were, in those days, several wash houses in Evenley and these were also bake houses. They each had a copper and large oven that could be heated by burning thorn faggots of wood and these were the places where the Club dinner was cooked. The meat and Yorkshire puddings and the vegetables were cooked here and carried along to the barn piping hot. After dinner, there were sports for the men, women and children. There were roundabouts, swings, hoop-la, coconut shies and other attractions at night assembled on the Green for the occasion and this was well attended by the folk from Brackley and other neighbouring villages and so ended a great day for Evenley in those years.

The Seamy Side
There were other stories told of those times and some that perhaps should be forgotten—how boys were whipped for insolence and for not doing their work properly and a stone or clod of earth thrown at them while driving the plough teams for the ploughman.

'Drumming out' was practised all round the district. If a couple were living together as man and wife and were not married or not conforming to the laws of society, they were drummed out of the villages or places where they lived by beating buckets and tin cans with sticks and giving them no peace at night outside the places or houses where they lived until they moved out. As no one else would have these people, most of them became tramps from place to place for the rest of their lives,

THE SCHOOL
Evenley School and Evenley Church played a very important part in the life of Evenley in those years and it can only be realised by those who lived

in Evenley at this period. School life started at the age of three years, in the infant school for two years and then we were taken into the main schoolroom until the age of thirteen, the end of school days. Mr. Charles Shelford was the Schoolmaster for boys and girls over five and Miss Wooton for the infant classes.

Evenley School

School started with the bell at nine a.m. followed by the register, prayers and hymn, accompanied by Mr. Shelford on the piano or violin and lessons proceeded until eleven o'clock, when there was a break of ten minutes in the playground. Then back to lessons until twelve o'clock, each boy or girl who lived close by going home to dinner. School began again at half past one until four o'clock, with a break of ten minutes at three o'clock. Friday ended the school week and every Friday afternoon after break the school song books were brought out and the week finished in singing the school song.

As the years went by each boy and girl moved up into a higher form or standard, as it was then called, until he or she reached the fourth. Then there was a sort out, some remaining in the fourth for another year the others going on until the seventh standard was reached by marks and an examination for that purpose.   So there were pupils who did not reach the seventh at all.

It was a mixed school and I should imagine that a big change has taken place in the schools of today.   It must have.   There were no student riots in my day.   The taxpayers would soon knock their grants off, sort 'em out and send 'em packing.   It makes my blood boil and thousands more of my generation.

The girls learned in standard just the same as the boys.   The boys sat at desks on one side of the school, running lengthwise and the girls together on the other side.   They were parted by a kind of passage down the centre of the school.   The desks were arranged for this purpose and each one sat in the same seat or place until the next year, day after day, so that the elder of the children sat all across the school in that order, coming down to the smaller children at the other end, in standards one to seven.   When a girl reached the fifth standard, she took different lessons from the boys. She attended sewing classes three times a week under the care of Mrs. Shelford, usually in the afternoons.   Girls did not do some of the boys' lessons at all.   By learning to knit and sew, many a girl learned to put heels in socks, a tricky operation, from Mrs. Shelford.

We were there to learn

It was made plain to all the pupils from the start that we were at school to learn.   If a boy transgressed at school, he felt the stick and it was no use to go home complaining for he had deserved it.

On Wednesday morning, lessons were taken in Scripture by the Rev. Edward Worsley, who attended the school for that purpose among the older pupils.

The County Council School Attendance Officer called from time to time to examine the school register and if there was much absenteeism, he called on the parents to know the reason why.   But there was very little absenteeism in those days.   There might have been because there were pupils who had to walk a long distance from Plomers Firs, Barley Mow, Knight's House and Monk's House farms and outlying places.

The Day's Round

It did not do for a boy or girl to enter the school during prayers, as these were said and they could be heard at the door. Instinct told them what to do and what not to do. Woe betide the boy who, by being thoughtless, did not take off his cap on entering. It did not do for a boy to defy Mr. Shelford. He was soon put in his place.

The school register was kept as each boy or girl entered and marked if he arrived by ten minutes past nine with a letter 'L' for late and after half past nine, 'A' for absent. In this case, he was allowed to enter, but it was a black mark for him on the register and it did not do to have too many 'As' against your name. One Evenley girl had an unbroken line of 'Ps' for perfect for four years, an astonishing performance and she is alive today and living on the outskirts of London.

And so lessons proceeded, with a lesson every day for a given time and other lessons daily in proportion. The school clock was kept in time and wound and attended to by Mr. Shelford and underneath the clock were the words: "Anything you have to do, do it well".

Sometimes things got rather noisy and appeared to be getting out of hand, due to all the pupils counting or repeating individually figures or words out loud to themselves more than they should. "Silence!" called the schoolmaster and the blackboard had a crack with his stick. That blackboard had more hidings than the boys. There was silence immediately and pointing to these few words he would say: "These words were not put here for decoration. Remember them. You all have your talents. Use them. Make less noise; proceed with your work". A pin could be heard to drop all over the schoolroom for days.

Close by was another framed picture at which no pointing was needed. Every boy and girl had learned them by heart, so that if any one of them—(they were One to Ten) - was asked for by anyone, they were promptly told correctly—The Ten Commandments. They had been said and heard in the Sunday School or Church Service so often that they were implanted in a boy's or girl's mind and at the Church service each one was followed by a Kyrie chanted by the choir, singing: "Lord have mercy upon us and incline our hearts to keep his law", words from the school motto downwards that could have never been forgotten. But today, if anyone asked a boy "Tell me the Fifth and Eighth Commandments" nine out of ten would say "Dunno, I never heard of 'em". I have tried it with my own boys and others who have been to school in Brackley. Well, Well! No wonder the police courts and jails are full.

I enjoyed Lessons

I lapped up Geography and History, Natural and English, like a hungry dog. Why? That's the question. It was an obsession, a talent given to me and I used it. I have found it useful to me all these years, but it was more or less hidden. It has now blossomed and is coming out to fruition, otherwise I should never have tackled this job at my age. I trust I shall be able to finish it in a right and proper manner. It is the kind of job I always wanted to do, for the pen is mightier than the sword. Enough said. There was another boy being schooled with me at Evenley, three years or so younger. He was getting the words in just the same manner. He was to become a policeman and rise to the rank of Superintendent.

One might ask "What has all this twaddle to do with it"? It is like a gigantic jigsaw puzzle for all my generation to have a go at. All of them have seen what I have seen, the changes that have come about wherever they are living, some more so than others, depending on their age, from their living places and looking at it from a different angle. I had to make a start somewhere, like Lord Mountbatten, so that is where Evenley comes into the picture with my school days and onwards through life. This great gentleman was living as it were, in my life and all of my generation, but there was this difference—whereas he saw a great Empire at its best and its trials going downhill, I was seeing all this at the same time and in the same way from my native home in Evenley.

The Diary and the Map

A diary was kept by the schoolmaster for several years. He would sometimes say to a boy or girl, "Will you fill the diary in"? Yes, there it was—dated; wind direction, state of weather, weekly rainfall, taken by the Vicar from his rain gauge. I did this for him several times. It was a job for the Seventh Standard and if anything worth noting had taken place, this was put down also and it was initialled. Sometimes I told my father

50

Schoolchildren on the Green

an inch of rain had fallen on a certain day the previous week. He did not know this, but he knew the ground was soaking.

The school map was something worth looking at. It was about five feet square, the Army Ordnance Map of the Parish of Evenley. There it was, in every detail, its boundary including the county boundary, all its houses, buildings and outhouses, the Church, the trig. points, the woods, coniferous and deciduous, its waterways and watershed, contours, fields in acres and fractions.

Every year a civilian gentleman would call at twelve o'clock punctually at the school, which was emptied quickly for these gentlemen to work on the parish map and compare it with their own. They were the Army Ordnance Survey Map Surveyors, going round with their equipment to visit every trig. point in all the area, in other parishes as well, coming into the nearest railway station and going away in the same way. I learned where the trig. points were to be found at Evenley from Mr. Shelford. Some were marked by a broad arrow. They can be found in every parish church and on certain gateposts. There is one on Evenley Church.

Sometimes Mr. Shelford would take the map down and place it on the blackboard with all the seventh standard boys. The girls would be sewing. He would put his ruler on one particular field or plot and divide it up and as he did so would call out in chains, poles or perches, so many in length and width.   This was written down by the boys to find out how much ground there was by working it out to find the answers.   I did not know at the time, but one night when waiting for the choir practice after I had left school, he told me we had worked out a problem and many others like these in one way or another by square and long measure for the Parish Council.   Farmers and labourers, hoeing, thatching and ploughing, drilling and ditching - many men were paid in this way.

A lot of piece work and contract work was done in those days.   He had given us a job to the benefit of the parish of Evenley.   Whether other parishes had these jobs worked out for them likewise, I never knew.   I suppose they had, for all villages came under their own Parish and County Council in this way.   I learned the names of the fields, plots and parcels at school by working in this way.   Compulsory education had come to all counties.

The Policeman Calls

After a few words with Mr. Shelford, he called out, "I want to see So and So and So and So and So and So, in their family names and these boys were sent out to him in that order until all the oldest boys in the school were lined up under the wall of the playground.   We knew what he had come from and he promptly showed us why.   There were two boys who went out of the door laughing and he dealt them a blow with his helmet and said for all to hear "This is no laughing matter, my lads"! Laughter turned to tears immediately.

An orchard at Evenley had been raided during the dinner hour the day before and most of the boys had gone into school with their pockets full of apples and Mr. Shelford had no option but to have all the apples taken out of their pockets and lined them up on the school window ledges.   It looked like Harvest Festival in the school.   Some boys had not been there. That did not matter.   He had got the lot that were there and that was the matter that concerned him.

It was not because of the stolen apples that the policeman called; it was the damage done, breaking the branches and shaking the apples on the ground that he had come about.   After a good ticking off, we were allowed to go back in school, promising never to let it happen again.

I write this because my generation was full of mischief and no different from any generation, before or after. There was this difference, however and that was that we had to keep our distance or put up with the consequences—a crack with a stick or a smack of the ear with the hand, even six weeks afterwards and perhaps another hiding from our fathers when they got to know what had happened. It was no use complaining that we had had a tanning. Those were the days when the punishment fitted the crime. So much different today. We were taught at school never to interfere by word or deed with a postman, policeman or parson.

Helping the Caretaker

A school caretaker came in every morning to light the fires and see that a fire was going and everything in order at half past eight. There was a rota of boys to bring in the coal, two boys one day and two the next and so on throughout the week. These, the eldest and strongest boys, were excused prayers and carried in the coal for the infants' room as well, holding the handle of the scuttle on either side as low as possible and so every boy carried in the coal at some time or another. At four o'clock the caretaker would come in again for cleaning purposes, to bring in wood and coal if necessary to light the fires in the morning.

Holidays

The holidays were taken by the older boys at Easter, planting potatoes and again at harvest, leading the horses, bringing in the harvest and at cricket on the Green, when a sixpenny piece would be placed on the middle stump for any boy who could bowl out Mr. Shelford or another Evenley man who was also a school teacher in London and who spent his holidays with his parents in Evenley. The cricket bats and other gear were given to the school by the Men's Cricket and Football Club.

There was a prize giving day when the lucky ones, first, second and third for different classes, received a book from the Rev. Worsley.

When the boys and girls left school, usually on a Friday, the afternoon was taken up by singing the school songs, picked out by the ones who were leaving and so the school days, weeks and years passed by.

So I was able to study at school or home by reading the paper, for when school ended for the day, that was it. A boy or girl did not bring back work from school in my day, for the simple reason that there was not room for him or her to write in peace, for most of the cottages had one to six in the family, coming along one by one. My memory was sharpened up in this way.

The Schoolmaster

Mr. Shelford was a good schoolmaster at Evenley and none of his pupils could say other of him who passed their schooldays with him. He taught music, played the piano and violin and was the organist and choirmaster at Evenley Church for approximately fifty years and what he said was law. There were several boys played truant and I was one of them. Brackley Fire Brigade had gone tearing up the Hinton Road, horse driven, to a hay rick fire. All the boys that could run left Evenley School at dinner time to be there, leaving only the girls at school for afternoon lessons. There was a rare ticking off for the lot of us who had played truant when we attended school next morning. There was no more playing truant in my time.

THE CHURCH

From a picture of Evenley Church prior to 1865 that hung in the vestry of the present church, it looked almost identical to the churches of Croughton and Hinton-in-the-Hedges, a strongly built church with a tower, possibly Norman or Saxon in origin. Almost all records of Evenley in early times perished in a fire that gutted the church entirely. It is said that the Church was filled with hay, there being no services held at that time. As there were many who could neither read nor write, services were of no avail.

The Church was rebuilt in 1865 by the Hon. Mrs. Pierrepoint of Evenley Hall in memory of her husband. It is said that it cost £2000 and that they saw to it that the people of Evenley attended regularly afterwards. A spire and a belfry with a peal of bells were added and as such is Evenley Church today, now in the diocese of Peterborough and merged with Croughton.

Candles provided light in the Church for a great many years, until 1910, when gas was used from Brackley gasworks after having been brought down from Evenley Hall to the Middle Farm where a gas engine was used for grinding and chaff cutting purposes to feed the stock that were housed under cover in the buildings of Middle Farm. Gaslight was used for the first time for a confirmation service taken by the Bishop of Peterborough that year and was a wonderful improvement for the Church, taking the place of candle light. This was undertaken by instructions from Major W.H. Allen, owner of Evenley Hall and its estate at that time.

Hot water radiators provided heating for the Church for a great number of years. A coke boiler heated the water and this was in sole use until paraffin heaters were installed. These heaters were not much improvement. The coke fired boiler and hot water radiators were very good if they were attended to regularly. The Church clock was wound and oiled regularly from 1900 to 1914, chiming the quarter hours and striking the hours through these years.

The Church

Services

The services at St. George's Church were Matins at eleven o'clock, Evensong at six, with Communion after Matins every third Sunday. The services were taken by the Rev. Edward Worsley and when one of his sons was at home, he would read the lessons.

The Choir

Evenley Church had during these years a strong choir of twelve boys, the best voices of Evenley School, taken at eight years to sing in the choir until his voice was broken, from thirteen to sixteen.   He then learned to sing alto and took his place in the men's seats, later to become a tenor or bass, according again to his voice.   So Evenley choir comprised twelve boys, soprano; four alto; four tenors; six baritone or basses, all taking their places, cantori or decani.   Now and again an Evenley choir man living away would attend and a place would be found for him in the choir, with a great welcome.

Mr. Shelford was organist and he trained the choir.   The organ was blown manually at this time and he trained one boy at a time to blow the organ regularly for him for a period of years.   Choir practice was at seven every Thursday night in the school, unless there were holidays, then the choir practice on Thursdays was discontinued during the holidays.   Also there was a Choir practice at five until a quarter to six pm. In the School on Sunday evening, when the chants for the psalm and hymn tunes for Evensong were gone through.   An anthem was practised and sung in the Church on Easter Day, Whitsun, Harvest Festival and Christmas Day and on these days Evenley choir was sustained by several ladies singing alto. On these days were processions, when it was dry, from the vestry and down the aisle from the front door to their places in the choir, robed in freshly washed and ironed surplices.

Evenley choir was strong enough to tackle the Hallelujah Chorus and other choruses from Handel's Messiah and here I should like to pay tribute to Mr. Charles Shelford.   He was a truly remarkable man, dedicated to his work at Evenley and a friend to old and young alike, with a lifelong service to the parish of Evenley.   Also, Mrs. Shelford, by taking a class for knitting and sewing with the girls three afternoons a week. When Mr. Shelford died in 1935, Evenley lost a great friend.   He had been Schoolmaster at Evenley School and had been Organist and

Choirmaster at Evenley Church for fifty years and had given a dedicated life service to the parish of Evenley. He was respected and loved by old and young alike, living out his retirement at Evenley.

EMPLOYMENT AND FARMING

Employment at Evenley was agriculture, chiefly arable. When boys left school, most were taken on the farms and employed by the local farmers and some worked on the same farm where their fathers were working. There was no other work for a boy to learn a trade as is the case today. When a boy was eighteen years, there was the Navy, Army and Police Force and he was a lucky boy to join the Police Force. He had to have an unblemished character, height five feet ten in his socks, good general character and fit in mind and body. Much the same thing applied to those boys to join the Navy and Army. There were two, however, that managed to do it that I knew as boys at Evenley School, one into the Grenadier Guards in 1912, the other into the Royal Navy in 1914.

The wages at this time were two and six weekly for boys starting work from school and that is the wage I received when I left school. The daymen's wages were twelve shillings weekly and the horsemen (carters and stockmen) thirteen shillings weekly, with a shilling a week extra for Sunday work to attend their animals, horses, cattle and sheep on Sundays. This was general around the adjoining counties. There were many families brought up on twelve to thirteen shillings weekly and with three, four, five or six children kept clean in clothes and fed in those days and going to school happy and clean.

In a census I took part in at school, there were sixty nine children going to school in 1911 at Evenley and the average was from sixty five to seventy during my schooldays.

Although the hours were long and the work heavy and tough, men and boys went walking to work, cheerful and happy and contented with their lot for such low wages. They still found time for recreation and to attend to their families' needs, working their gardens and allotments.

WORKING ON THE LAND

There were a large number of men and boys employed in agriculture at this time, not only in Evenley, but all over the counties, as agriculture took up most of the labour force.   Most farms of around two hundred acres employed approximately ten men and boys and so on some farms they had a labour force from ten to twenty.   The day of the tractor had not arrived and horse work was the chief power—ploughing, harrowing and mowing and reaping by horses.   There were carters (horsemen), stockmen, shepherds and daymen to fit the needs of the farms.

The hours of work were long.   The daymen, who worked a lot on contract and did no Sunday work, worked from seven am to four pm if they had their luncheon break at midday out in the fields and seven to five if they came home to dinner, from Monday to Saturday.   The carters and stockmen started work at five in the morning and had to feed and groom the horses.   Then back to breakfast at half past six and back to their stables at seven to harness the horses and start out to work on the farms at seven thirty.   There was a break of half an hour at midday and then they brought their horses at three o'clock to give them their water and feed before going home to their own dinner.   Then they returned to the farms to groom and feed their horses again and make them comfortable for the night, usually finishing their day at six pm.   There were no Saturday afternoons for men working on farms in those years.

Mattie Buggins & Winnie Hosford

Sheep

Most farms had their flocks of sheep and in some cases father and son were shepherds. The wages and hours were much the same for these as the carters and stockmen. The sheep were penned on the ploughland, feeding on mustard, turnips, kale, hay and swedes throughout the winter months. They got very dirty and in April and May were driven in flocks across the Green on their way down to Washbrook at the New Pond where they were washed ready for shearing during the month of May.

Leslie with pet sheep on the Green

Milk and Eggs

Several farms had their own dairy herds of four to twenty milking cows and these supplied the local needs of milk and butter. The milk was sold at the farms fresh daily what was needed, the remainder being turned by churning into butter and finding its way into the grocers shops at Brackley. Fowls were kept on free range in rickyards on most farms and usually there were plenty of fresh eggs available cheaply and pickled for use when they were scarce.

Grain

Most of the corn that was planted in these years was hand-sown and then harrowed and ploughed in. There were teams of bullocks for a lot of the work. My father said, as a boy, he drove a bullock team which was about the last in Evenley and that they were ploughing in the South

Ground, now a covert, and one day when it was very hot they gadded and ran away, smashing the plough and harness and when they were found not a bit of tackle was left on them. They were in the shade of the Ash Beds, another covert on the estate.

The corn was threshed out with a flail with two men threshing in a barn throughout the winter and spring daily. The corn was mown or reaped with a scythe and sickle by the men and then it was tied up and stooked by the rest of the families, all playing their part at harvest time. Some farms had their own set of threshing tackle and some engaged a contractor. The corn was sent to Brackley Mill and mills at Banbury and Buckingham, to be turned into flour and then brought back to the bakeries and most villages around the district had their own bakery where it was baked and made into bread.

The Coming of Machinery

During 1890 to 1900, there were many changes. Most farms now had their own threshing machines worked by steam, mowing machinery for hay and a self deliverer for corn. This machine cut the corn and gathered it and swept the corn with four large rakes from a platform into sheaves on the ground, to be tied up by hand after it was cut. Plough, harrows and drags and other equipment changed for the better quickly. Drills, carts and wagons improved yearly. There were elevators for making hayricks and these were driven by a pony geared to a pole and walking round and round in a circle to turn the gear to drive the elevator.

There were contractors who owned sets of ploughing tackle visiting the farms and helping out with ploughing and cultivating. These all had the roughest land to clean and were kept busy all summer, from daylight to dark, working mostly on the fallow land and most farms had their fields of fallow.

There were two huge fifteen ton steam engines one on either side of the fields with huge drums carrying a wire rope cable, winding and then unwinding, drawing a six furrow balance plough or cultivator to and fro across the field until the job was completed. Water had to be carted by horse and water cart to these while they were working to keep up their steam pressure and this meant a long day for horses and man with the water cart doing this job.

The first farm tractors to make their appearance were very heavy and at first not a great success. They were unable to work on the land in the winter months and the work they did could not compare with the steam ploughing for which they were intended. They started on petrol and then ran on paraffin. The ploughs were heavy and did not do their work properly. However, they were the first tractors to work on paraffin for farm work and came from Government International Tractors in America.

During the years 1905 to 1912, came another invention, the self binder. Two firms specialised in these machines, the Hornsby and the Jones. The machines cut and tied the corn with string, throwing out the tied up sheaves as it was drawn round and round the field with three horses until the piece of corn was finished cutting at the centre of the field. Most farms acquired one of these machines and the self deliverer was put aside and not used any more, gradually becoming a museum piece of equipment. The binder speeded up harvest very fast and made it a lot easier for master and men in these years. There was still some scything done, however, for if the corn was flattened and twisted by rain and storms, there were patches that had to be cut out and tied as before and these machines could not do their work in these conditions.

In the harvest of 1935 a new machine made its appearance, the combine harvester, to cut and thresh our corn in one operation. It was the first of many and in time was to revolutionise harvesting operations. It had one drawback—it could only work when the corn was dry and in good condition. The corn dryer had not made its appearance but this was something new from Canada.

The new farm tractors were not being fitted with rubber tyres for working in summer and dry conditions and this meant changing wheels when the going was wet and greasy and most farm tractors had two sets of wheels for this purpose. Rubber tyres were to be improved in later years, until iron wheels were discarded altogether.

More and more dairying was being done and most farms were producing milk and there were larger flocks of sheep, suited to grassland, of the Border Leicester breed.

Bill on a tractor

Many acres of land were laid down at this period. The number of horses engaged in agriculture was now down to a minimum. The farm tractor was doing the bulk of the work on farms and less labour was required. Some farms took up pig breeding and feeding for the bacon factories that were now producing bacon cured for the home market. The breed of pigs were chiefly Large Whites and Middle Whites.

Working for the Big House

Some of the boys were taken and employed as gardeners in the big estate houses of the neighbourhood. Some houses had a staff of six to eight gardeners to deal with the greenhouses, vegetable gardens, lawns and flower beds and most farm houses had a gardener, full time or otherwise. Most estates employed one or two keepers and these looked after the game birds. There were some boys who started work in the stables of the big houses as stable boys, to become grooms for the hunting horses, nags and ponies and there were many of these for one purpose or another. There was a lot of hunting with the Bicester or Grafton packs of hounds at this time and these men trained their own horses.

WATER SUPPLY AND SEWERAGE

Water Supply

A plentiful underground water supply at Evenley could be found almost anywhere by the sinking of artesian wells from thirty to forty feet deep. Most of the cottages drew their water from several wells around the village for a great number of years and most of the farms had their own wells. Water was pumped with a lead pump at a lot of places and at other places drawn by a windlass, chain and bucket. There would be one well that served several cottages and it was a job for most mothers and older boys of that time to draw and carry the water into their homes and into the houses of the elderly and those unable to do it. The young children were not allowed to go near the wells.

There were three springs at Evenley also that never had been known to fail during the hottest summer, where a bucket could be filled at surface level with good, clean spring water quickly. These were at Hedge Meadow, the Spring and Stockwell. There was plenty of water, but it meant work for someone to get it. But it was cheerfully enough done in those days. During the dry summers the water would get a bit in short supply and rather low in the wells. There were then trips to these three places to fill and carry buckets of water for drinking purposes.

Brackley had its own waterworks and had a very deep well that supplied most of the town with water piped round to serve its needs.

In the year 1905, a great improvement came to Evenley that was of real benefit to the cottages and people. Major Allen's father, known as the Old Squire, had, at his own expense, a deep well of approximately seventy feet sunk, together with a reservoir and erected a windmill pump over the well in the Backside field to provide all his tenanted cottages with water. Pipes were laid all round the village and stand pipes were set up that supplied one, two or more cottages with water near the doors of the cottages merely by lifting a handle. The smallest child could draw water now, if having the strength to lift the handle. No longer was it necessary to go to the wells for water and so many wells were filled in and not used any more that they were no longer a source of danger and worry to mothers with young children.

The Old Squire, William Allen, died in the following year, in 1906, so perhaps he did not live long enough to see this work come into operation.

The wind pump supplied Evenley for approximately fifty years and stood until recently without its wheel, showing the direction of the wind only and acting as a large weather vane by its tail fin. Like most things, it served its purpose for as long as could be needed, serving Evenley people with a good supply of good, clean drinking water.

Sewage Disposal

Like most villages around, Evenley's sewage was a primitive problem. Most cottages had an earthen closet and this was shared in most cases by two families. These closets were cleaned out, from the outside, twice a year, in spring and autumn and it was not a very nice job for the fathers of the families of that time. This operation was carried out at night by the light of a full moon after all the children had gone to bed. A three or four hours' job with a wheelbarrow to get it out of the way and this meant a long day for someone in those days and years. In 1903 and 1908 this problem received the attention of the Young Squire, Major W.H. Allen and at his own instructions and expense he caused a closet to be built, one to each family and supplied each one with a bucket. This enabled these closets to be cleaned out more regularly, once a week or less. This was a major improvement to the old system in use at Evenley and elsewhere.

It is well that some of these things should be remembered, for there were no grants by the Government for improvement to property and the rates did not cover so much in those years. When improvements were made, it was at the landlord's and squire's expense, for when a man's weekly wage was twelve to thirteen shillings, it needed all this for the upkeep of his family. No extra charges for rent for cottages were made for these improvements in 1900 to 1914. They remained static at two shillings to two and sixpence throughout these years.

During the nineteen-fifties, water was piped through the district from Buckingham and the village water supply was cut off. Evenley with other places close to Brackley was now supplied with water from the Bucks Water Board A larger sewage and disposal plant was built at Evenley and most of the cottages were connected to it.

Grants were now available for all properties with vacant cottages in fairly good order to provide hot water, bath and toilet facilities and a few were to be demolished altogether. Many owners took advantage of the grants and brought their properties into an up to date, modernised condition at this time.

SPORT AND AMUSEMENT

Cricket and Football

Evenley and many other villages around made their own amusement in much the same manner as other places. Cricket was the main sport for men and boys in the summer and for the mothers and daughters there were dancing, singing and whist drives. There was no bingo.

Football was played when the light was enough during September and October and again in February, March and April and during the Christmas holidays. There were enough men and boys to form three teams. A lot of it was played on the Green, although the road ran through the centre, making it awkward, but nobody seemed to mind and cricket went on as though the road did not exist.

There was a cricket field at Evenley Hall and the best cricket was played here. Evenley and the neighbouring villages had strong cricket clubs and a team would be chosen among masters and men and the men were allowed time off to play. The matches started at three o'clock on Saturdays.

All the cricket and football matches were what was called friendly matches in those days. The League matches of today had not begun. Great rivalry existed between Brackley, Turweston, Syresham, Croughton, Aynho, Charlton, King's Sutton, Mixbury and Hinton-in-the-Hedges. All of them had a cricket club and played one another at home and away in turn..

There were gentlemen farmers playing with these village teams and most of them allowed their men time off away from their work to be able to start these cricket matches on time at three o'clock on Saturdays. They also provided their men with transport by pony and trap, cobs and cabs and other horse-drawn vehicles. There were many of these. The motor had not yet arrived. After playing friendly and league cricket matches in the cricket field at Evenley Hall for a great number of years, Evenley Cricket Club, in 1939, had to find another place to play cricket and a wicket was obtained for matches and practice in the Church Leys for several following years, until it returned to the Green.

Cricket at Evenley Hall

Quoits
Some of the men played quoits and many of the public houses had their own beds. The beds were made by digging two holes in the ground so far apart and filling them with clay soil and then topped with turf. The idea was to pitch their quoits on a feather approximately fifteen yards apart. Each team had a skip to tell them how far and near to the feather they were and to see if they could knock out of the ground their opponent's quoit. Scoring was much the same as for bowls. When it was wet in the summer and too wet for cricket, the quoits were brought out and played on the Green for practice and to save the quoit beds from over use. The Red Lion at Evenley had a quoit bed in the Red Lion Close. Quoits have gone out of favour and are no longer played in Evenley.

Dancing and Whist
In Evenley and most other places there were plenty of men and women who could play a musical instrument well, of one kind or another. There

were many good violinists and players of the organ and piano in the district, as well as performers on the concertina and melodia. Many families had the humble harmonium that had been in the family for generations.

When it was fine in the summer, mostly on festival days and holiday times, there were men at Evenley, two especially, who brought out their instruments and sat under one of the nine elm trees on the Green at this time and began to play. It was the signal for a dance. My mother, with other mothers of the day, put on a clean apron quickly and was very soon out there with them. Yes, daughters as well and old time dancing was going full swing. The lancers, quadrilles and other dancing, all in good tempo. They were joined by some of the men folk, spruced up in their best clothes of that time and the younger boys and girls sat down around them, looking at their fathers, mothers and sisters with great interest and the grandmothers and others sat in chairs in the open doorways of their cottages, enjoying the scene just as much as if they were dancing themselves. There were intervals and immediately young and old alike would be singing songs like 'Keel Row' and 'Who Killed Cock Robin'? And other songs that they all knew by heart. There was no need for song books and so many mothers spent what was for them an enjoyable evening.

In the winter months, there were lots of whist drives at Evenley and other places within walking distance. They were arranged so that they did not clash with whist drives at Brackley, Mixbury, Cottisford, Croughton or Hinton-in-the-Hedges.

Leisure Time has Changed

The pattern of life was the same all round the neighbourhood, from Buckingham, Bicester, Towcester and Banbury. Very little was heard of horse racing, betting or gambling. and bingo—well, for that one would have to look in a dictionary to see what it meant, if ever the word was said or heard. I myself did not hear the word 'bingo' until after World War Two. But life was changing fast every year, in some ways for the better and in some ways for the worse. There were no games played and no boisterous singing to be heard on Sunday and for a boy to kick a ball on Sunday was simply asking for a stern rebuke from someone other than his parents. Sunday was kept for what it was intended.

There was a certain amount of Sunday work that had to be done and only the necessary work was done and this as quietly as possible and that was the feeding and attention of animals. There was only the barking of a dog or perhaps a cry of "Fire" to disturb the peace.

There were some families, however, who had brothers and sisters, mostly married, living in their own homes at Brackley and close by, who would meet on a Sunday evening in the homes of their parents. The harmonium would be drawn out and Songs of Praise could be heard, Hymns A & M and Methodist and Moody and Sankey tunes after evensong at Church, approximately half past seven to nine pm. I enjoyed these parties as a boy of twelve and looked forward to the next time. Those were the days when there was good singing in harmony. People did not like to sing in unison in those days and years and if they could not sing these tunes and the words properly and with feeling, then they did not sing them at all.

We Walked in Those Days

Some parents with young children took them for a walk on Sunday evening down Mill Lane by the woods of Evenley to the river Ouse and its railway bridges to watch the trains go by and look at the water. There was so much in those days to interest them. This was the favourite walk, coming back through the woods and on the footpath back home or vice-versa. There were others walking out from Brackley or back to Brackley from Evenley via Evenley Park. There were a lot of people walking it in this way on various walks. Evenley had well trodden footpaths and bridle roads with their gates and stiles in good order and no barbed wire was to be seen. The hunting people did not like it and took good care of this. The hedges and fences were kept in good order by the aid of the billhook and posts and rails.

It was said in an article in the Times that Brackley had the finest entrance to a town in the Midlands in these years. From Evenly crossroads on the road leading to Oxford and Northampton through

Brackley, now known as A43, was an avenue of large beech trees. These trees covered the whole of the road and its grass verge to the parish boundary, the river Ouse, approximately a hundred yards into the town of Brackley, about one and a quarter miles. They were so thick that when the sun was at its height and the trees were in full leaf in summer, no sunlight could get through except when an odd branch or two had blown off during a gale. This avenue of beech trees had criss- cross iron chains and wedges to keep them together. They must have been hundreds of years old and had trunks five feet through their centres. They were the home of the red squirrel and these could often be seen crossing the road or jumping or sitting on the branches

The Oxford Road from Brackley to Evenley was a lovely walk and many people came this way in the summer. The trees formed a boundary of the Evenley Park lands and were part of the Evenley Hall estate. Alas, the trees have all gone except two as they had become a hazard to traffic.

In those days the American grey squirrel or tree rat was not known or seen. But today there is not a single red squirrel to be seen in the district. They have all gone. The tree rat is everywhere now. What a change in sixty years.

Organ Grinders and Bands

The barrel organ grinder, together with the barrel organ and monkey, could be frequently seen going round the Green, stopping at intervals to play and the children of Evenley throwing their pennies to the monkey with great laughter and delight.

There were several good local brass bands in the district. Brackley Town Band and Brackley Salvation Army Band and others came to play their music on Evenley Green

Occasionally another band came into Evenley, to stop like the organ grinder round the Green. They would come into the village and gather up what coppers they could by playing their instruments, then with their gutteral 'Danke sehr', bowing and scraping, disappear as quickly as they came. They were men of around fifty years of age by their appearance, usually six in number. They all wore spectacles and a long dark coat, even during the hottest days of summer.   They were never seen without their long coats.   They seemed well dressed with highly polished shoes and each wore a peculiar type of hat, brown in colour and all much alike in shape and design.   They certainly were not tramps.   Their instruments were highly polished and their music was excellent.   They carried no extra baggage for food or clothing.   Where did they sleep or feed?   They interfered with no one.   They moved around the countryside quickly from place to place, on foot for they had no transport with them and the money they earned by their music would not pay for their shoe leather.

Were these gentlemen from Germany doing this for the love of it?   It seemed so.   Yet it did not seem to fit in with the English way of life somehow.   They seemed so mysterious and no one could supply the answer and never did, then or up to now.   They could travel by train backward and forward to London every day, for there was a good train service.

I saw them several times between 1910 and 1912.   But one day during the summer of 1912, I was home from school during dinner time and I saw a strange sight.   Three policemen walked about fifty yards apart. Each policeman had on either side of him two of these German gentlemen and were escorting them handcuffed across Evenley Green towards Brackley.

Well, well! What had they been doing to be taken away like this?   No one seemed to know, but it was the last visit of the German Bands.   They had come to England to work for a purpose and they had not been seen or heard of in this country since.   Although Evenley folk did not know, a dark cloud was to appear over the horizon. 'Kaiser Bill was on the move'.

Kaiser Bill

70

ELECTRICITY COMES TO EVENLEY

Electrical energy had been used in the larger towns in various forms for years and many of the large country houses had their privately owned electrical lighting plants. Petrol and gas driven engines worked dynamos to charge batteries. A few plants were also wind driven for the same purpose. In the early 1930's plans were made to link up the country on the electricity grid system and so in time Evenley had a supply of electricity. It was brought in from Northampton via Buckingham and Brackley to Evenley by land line during 1932-34 by the East Midlands Electric Light Company.

Most of the cottages and the Church were wired for lighting at this time and this was a big improvement on the paraffin lamps. After the wiring came cookers and other heating appliances. Electric cookers were installed by the Company to those who needed them and these were at first paid for by instalments on the quarterly light bill, perhaps the first of the hire purchase system of today.

Most households did their cooking previously over a kitchen range with a coal and wood fire, open or closed in the fireplace. The iron kettles, saucepans and boilers were always to be seen. No fire was wasted for the heating of water. It was a hot job for the mothers of families of that time to prepare and cook meals in the middle of summer, as a fire was necessary all the year around, winter and summer.

All this was finished with the electric cooker and these became a must, most households buying one. There were also aluminium utensils to be bought to replace the old kettles and iron boilers and life was a lot easier for the housewife, being cleaner and more pleasant with the use of electricity and as time went by, less coal and wood was needed.

New radio appliances were also coming on the market in large numbers. The all mains receiver could be plugged into wall sockets and so the wet battery charged wireless receivers were discarded for something new.

COMMUNICATIONS

Rail

With the coming of the railways a man and his family were able to travel, either for leisure or to seek other employment further afield and not to end his days in the same place as he probably would have done before 1860.

During the summers of 1910 to 1914, excursion trains would run to and from London, carrying many passengers on Sundays. Now and again there would be people coming from London to spend the day in and around the parklands of Brackley district and many visited Evenley Green and Evenley Park at these times. They enjoyed their day's outing very much, to sit under the trees and throw their pennies out for the village children to catch and to wear the boys' caps for an hour or so. They usually arrived about twelve o'clock and then going away about six to catch their train back to London and many of them liked a pint at the Red Lion. They liked a cup of tea too and would ask a boy to ask mother to make them a cup of tea. Soon a jug of tea was brought out with cups and when it was finished they would wrap silver coins in paper and return the cups and jug with money, saying "Give this to your mother and thank her for us". These people were well behaved and were very generous with their money and those who made tea for them were amply paid for their trouble.

Brackley Station

Getting about

Previous to the coming of the railways, the 'only communication of this vast area was the canal at Banbury and at Blisworth on towards London. All these places had their roads and in the winter time people must have had a terrible time to get about. I heard stories from the old men of Evenley that often a wagon would be travelling between Oxford and Northampton loaded and would sink up to the axles and be unloaded on the verge to enable the wagon to be moved and then loaded up again. Men were always digging stone where it was handy to that particular road to patch them up as well as they could and today these quarries may be seen in various fields round the neighbourhood.

The nearest point to Brackley for coal was at Aynho wharf and this place was always full of horses, vehicles and men drawing coal and other stuff from the barges. Some men did nothing else but this for a good many years of their lives and so perhaps that is where the Bad Old Days originated. What a relief and a blessing it must have been for the folk when the LMS Railway Company drove its branch line between Banbury and Bletchley and Banbury and Northampton. Then, in 1898 the Great Central Railway Company opened its main line from London to Rugby, all during the last hundred years. Now both are closed and disused. The branch line between Banbury and Bicester, built and opened in 1910, was the last railway to be built in this area and so opened up the large part of South Northamptonshire and North Oxfordshire.

During the year 1909, sounds of the blasting and shattering of the rock at Audley during the building of the Great Western Railway's new branch line from Banbury to London via Bicester could be heard at Evenley. This line opened in 1910 and so completed the railway network of the district, to spread its tentacles more or less over the whole country. Its blessing were felt everywhere, carrying coal, corn and straw and everything was moving so fast, bringing all commodities almost on the doorstep. Yes and desecration as well. Those fine old oak trees, elms, ash, beech and larch were being felled and loaded on special railway timber wagons daily. Many men of the district had left the land to build this railway and as their wages had a substantial increase, most of these men were lost to agriculture for good. Yes, those men and trees were lost to agriculture, never to return.

In the early 1930's a diesel train service was inaugurated on the LMS railway between Bletchley and Banbury for a time. This was discontinued owning to competition with motor cars and buses, to the detriment of the railway company and their Brackley railway station closed for passenger traffic, but remained open a little longer for goods traffic. Steam locomotives were still running on the line up to 1950.

Road

The horse still held his or her place in all this and was supreme by right, but horses and their drivers were probably at their best from 1910 to 1914. There were frequent runaways by the younger horses, for they did not like the puffing, chuffing, hissing monsters, the steam traction engines on rail or road. The goods yards of the railways at Brackley and other stations around were having runaways almost daily due to the clanging and banging of the wagons by the shunting engines to and fro in their sidings.

As the horses were being ridden, driven or walking at their work, they would probably sometimes meet hissing steam monsters along the country roads, the ploughing and threshing engines with all their gear and tackle cluttering up the whole road as they moved from farm to farm.

The drivers of these engines were very good and would stop to help the horses and drivers to pass by, but the younger horses easily took fright, shying and jumping and took some holding at these meetings. There was always steam, oil and smoke from these engines when they were stationary. There were plenty of horses that were almost as fresh after a day's work as when they set out in the morning, not an easy job for the boys, carters and horsemen after a hard day's work. Then perhaps they would meet the steam engines whose drivers did not stop to let them pass by. This was worse than ever and so many horses took fright and bolted. I saw several of these runaways as a boy, with the children running off the road to safety, scattering like chaff in the wind instinctively. Yes, the horse was always uneasy when these smelly things were about. The County Councils had their monster steam rollers working their districts, making another hazard for horse and horseman.

The hunting horses were much the same, looking as if they were ready to jump over anything or anybody. The tradesman's vans and pony carts were all the same. There were two places at Evenley where the ponies, cobs and vanners were trained by two horse breakers, one in the Red Lion Close and the other known as College Corner. Perhaps this is why College Corner got its name for training horses was known as 'Going to College'. Each of these places had a strong oak post set in the ground, carrying an iron ring like a swivel and the horses would be made to run on a length of strong rope round and round, tied to the post, by the crack of a whip or voice until they were mastered to stop or start at will.

The Bicycle and Tricycle

There were a few of these machines about in my early days, but it was only a few men or women that could afford to buy one, as money was scarce and a bicycle or tricycle was an expensive machine in these years. The postman at Evenley was a local man and he walked his rounds on foot, taking and picking up the mail from Brackley and with his wife he lived at Evenley and looked after the post office at his home. He was a man ageing in years and due to rheumatism he had to give up walking to Brackley in 1904. He continued to run the post office at Evenley for several years afterwards.

Penny Farthing by the Evenley Belle Coach House

A new postman now came to Evenley from Brackley. He wore GPO uniform as he came on his rounds and he rode a brand new bicycle, a dark red shining new bicycle and this red bicycle was the envy of every Evenley boy who were all longing to own and ride one like it. But where was the money to buy one? There was only one thing to do, to take their jackets off and work and save to get one and as the years went by, the bicycle became cheaper to buy and as the boys left school, a watch and a bicycle were the first things to be bought as soon as they had enough money to buy them. More and more second hand cycles came on the market and these were quickly snapped up as long as they were rideable and there were plenty of bikes without any brakes at all, but what matter—it was better than Shanks' pony.

Then in 1912 to 1914 the Brackley tradesmen, grocers and suchlike began to send their groceries from Brackley with a boy riding a tradesman's bicycle and delivering them to such of the people as were unable to walk into Brackley. There were also cycle shops in Brackley where a cycle could be hired for the day or longer if required. The tricycles of earlier years were fitted with solid tyres and became obsolete by 1914 and had gone like the penny farthing. I did not see one of these being ridden. And so the bicycle had come to stay for the next forty or fifty years as a means of transport.

The Petrol Engine

About 1908 another new kind of vehicle was seen chugging through Evenley, to and fro from Brackley, the first motor car and this also belonged to the Shelswell estate. Soon this one was joined by others owned by the landed gentry. These were mostly driven by trained chauffeurs at first, but as the year 1914 came there were quite a number of these vehicles on the roads and the motor car had come to stay to the present time, yet another means of transport, owner driven. The horse drawn coaches were soon to become a museum piece like a lot of things of their time. The petrol engine was soon to alter the lives of many a man by inventions and changes, for man was learning to fly like a bird and a few men had made a machine that did fly, if only for a short distance.

In 1936, work on the Oxford to Brackley A43 road being finished, cats eyes were built in the centre of the roadway, a useful invention for the safety of vehicles being driven at night and they were to be most valuable a few years later.

The Hot Air Balloon

Some men had given their attention to flying. They had been a considerable distance in balloons and seemed to be making great progress. They had been seen from Evenley, but not for a closer view, so when it became known that Bleriot was the first man to cross the Channel from Calais to Dover in an aeroplane in 1909, there was great excitement and the folk began looking into the skies to see if they could see anything of those strange looking contraptions. They did not have to wait very long for this either, for several were seen like the balloon at a distance by those who had good eyesight.

The First Aeroplane

The first aeroplane to be seen to land near Evenley was during September, 1912. "An aeroplane has landed at Mixbury" was the cry from mouth to mouth and everyone that could go was running, walking or driving towards Mixbury. Yes, there it was in a field between Mixbury and Finmere and near to the Great Central Railway and Mixbury Lodge and Plantation. It was a single seater monoplane and had to land owing to shortage of fuel. It seemed as though the whole population of the district had made their way to see it. The field was full of folk of all ages, rich and poor rubbing shoulders together. The plane was ringed by several policemen and no one was allowed to touch it. After a time, a motor truck arrived and this was also the first motor truck that had been seen and this was viewed as much as the aeroplane. Several mechanics inspected the machine and soon had it filled with fuel and oil. After clearing a passage way by the police, the engine of the plane was started by the propeller and in a few minutes the plane ran along the field and was gone like a bird into the air and was soon out of sight. This plane, the first in the area, was the forerunner of many more to come.

Between 1930 and 1934, flying was turning towards airship travel as a future passenger traffic. Most of the larger countries were now making and building these large dirigible airships. England had two, the R100 and the R101 and several smaller ones. It was a wonderful sight to see these airships on their trial flights. The R100 made a successful maiden flight to Canada and on its return flight it came over Oxford and Buckingham and the people of Evenley and others under its path had a ring side view of the cigar shaped monster, flying majestically homewards towards Cardington near Bedford. Now it was time for the R101 to make its maiden flight to India. This ended in disaster not long after taking off. The R101 struck a hilltop in France, caught fire and disintegrated with great loss of life. After other countries had their airship disaster, flying by airship was given up as being too hazardous an undertaking.

THE FIRST WORLD WAR

On August 4th 1914, Britain declared war on Germany, but at first it did not have much effect on the district and Evenley in particular. The bells rang out for Christmas and the New Year, but it was an uneasy Christmas. Thoughts were of the war and how long it was likely to last.

Early in the Spring of 1915, there was a call to arms and large posters appeared everywhere—"Your King and Country Need You, Join Kitchener's Army" and batches of young men flocked into the army as volunteers from every village and town in the country, followed by other batches and so the young men, from eighteen to forty, went off to the war from Evenley, Brackley and all the places round, squires, vicars' sons, policemen, postmen, shop men, agricultural labourers, railway workers in thousands. The local men mostly joined their own county regiments, the 7th Northamptonshire Regiment and the Oxon and Bucks Light Infantry. Some of the men joined the Royal Navy and what was then called the Flying Corps. Other men followed and were drafted into other regiments of the British Army and so Kitchener's Army became a massive force of volunteers from every walk of life.

Before long, there were only the old men and boys left to carry on with agriculture and many were the changes that took place from now onwards. The Women's Land Army was formed and many were the tasks the women had to do. Hay and straw were bought up and shipped to France to feed the army of horses and a body of women followed.

Recruiting Poster

A baler was driven by a steam engine to tie up and bind the hay and straw with wire, ready to be carried to the nearest railway goods yard for shipment to France. These bales were the first of their kind, the forerunners of the baler of today. They were heavy, cumbersome machines and they tied heavy bales that took two strong men to move them.

Pensions were now being paid at the rate of five shillings a week to people over seventy.

Prices of all commodities doubled from 1914 to 1916. Coal, foodstuffs, clothing, boots and shoes, everything was twice as dear and taxation began to make itself known.

There was a call too, to plant every bit of land with potatoes and other foodstuffs to help feed the country.

Hunting, county cricket and first class football were suspended during the duration of the war and other matters came under the Defence of the Realm Act.

Christmas, 1915 came round again, but it was a very quiet Christmas and altogether different from other Christmases. It had somehow lost its meaning. The bells were silent, being chimed only for the church services. Everything seemed to have gone wrong and so 1916 came in unheralded.

The War Drags on

In 1916 the war grew in intensity and fierceness. The daily papers printed large columns of the men who had lost their lives and many were the homes that were broken. All the places around, including Brackley, lost someone near and dear to them. Evenley lost two of its men in this year and great was the sorrow to hear the news. Both of these men were members of Evenley Church Choir. The war waged on in fierce and bitter struggle. Many changes had taken place in Evenley. Some of the farms had new tenant farmers, due to death and retirement. The bakery and wheelwright's shop at Evenley had ceased and the old was making way for something new.

Summer Time came into being on trial in 1916 and at first was not liked at all by the farming community and some farms still hung on to the old time for several years. Other farms went by the new time and this caused considerable confusion all round, but at this time it was not compulsory.

In 1917 the war was still dragging on. The casualty lists grew bigger and these were published in the daily papers of the day, of which there were now several available. Evenley lost two more men killed in action and others were badly wounded. A dark year for Evenley, whatever 1918 might bring.

By 1918 the aeroplane was a more familiar sight. These could be seen flying in the direction of Bicester and Heyford daily if it was fine. There were several bad crashes in the district, which drew many onlookers from the neighbourhood.

German prisoners of war were employed in batches on farms where they were needed and these were billeted in a house in Brackley. They were good workers and on the whole behaved well and gave no trouble. They had no thought for their Kaiser and cursed him for the mess they found themselves in.

There was also a VAD convalescent hospital for wounded men in Brackley. These men wore blue uniforms, some in bandages with sticks and others walking with crutches. In the daylight hours in summer there was a strange sight—German prisoners walking into their billet from work and passing on their way the wounded Tommies standing in the street and both parties giving friendly salutations as they passed each other. There

80

appeared to be no bitterness. They all seemed to have learned the cause of the war.

National Insurance and Pensions
The Act came into force in 1916 and all regular employees had to have a stamped card for sickness and pension benefit and with it most of the old village sick clubs ceased to operate. Evenley Sick Club ended at this time and most of its members joined the Oddfellows or Foresters Friendly Societies and these still operate at Brackley today.

Compulsory Service
This Act came into being in 1916. All men and single women from eighteen to fifty five years were now called up to report for service in some way or another and another great exodus of men from agriculture took place.

The 'Conchies'
Most places had one or two Conscientious Objectors and feelings for them were rather high. These men were not liked at all at this time. There were one or two altercations and many derisive remarks were made to them. But they had to face the music during their work and most of them drifted away from places to find a fresh home and work where they were unknown.

Wages
As the price of food increased, wages rose also and men on farms were earning about eighteen shillings weekly and were not so well off as they were before 1914.

The Cost to Evenley
As the summer of 1918 proceeded, there were rumours that the war might end. Prayers were said in the churches that it might be so. Sunday work was allowed again throughout the harvest season for five weeks and during this time Evenley lost its five men killed in action. On November 11th an armistice was called and for the time fighting ceased. The brewery

hooter blew its whistle for several hours of the day and there were tears of rejoicing. The German prisoners of war left their work at eleven o'clock and did not come back again. Peace was yet to be signed.

These five Evenley men gave their lives for their homes, King and country

Herbert George

Ernest Chatwell

Thomas Holton

Thomas Reynolds

Ernest Pratt

War

Memorial

In 1919 saw the signing of peace and the end of the war. Demobilisation started and the men returned to their homes and work slowly. But the pattern of life was now changed from pre-war years and for some a fresh start had to be made due to conditions.

Some of the farms had fresh owners and tenants and otherwise in the war years and these brought changes. Local Employment Exchanges were set up to help men find jobs and work where it was possible and gradually conditions became normal again.

Farming in War time

The labour force of the district was now reduced to older men and boys under 18, German prisoners, women folk and a few unfit soldiers here and there. There were many jobs that could not be done. The labour force was not strong enough or so skilful as formerly.

The winter to 1917 and the spring of 1918 were very wet with snow followed by rain, so that work on the land was difficult and behind for the planting and drilling of corn and in April and May Sunday work on the farms was encouraged, although it was not compulsory and consecutive weeks were worked without a break, to me at the time a thing that did not seem right, but necessary. All the acres that could be were ploughed and planted. There were many extra acres of potatoes planted than in former years in the district and the sets of steam ploughing tackle were going with a break throughout the summer.

Bread was rationed with other food stuffs at this time, but there appeared to be enough for all and this did not cause undue hardship. There was a rise in prices and wages, a third more than in 1914.

BETWEEN THE WARS

1919

From the autumn of 1919 until early 1920 a severe attack of influenza struck the whole country, taking away many thousands of people and most of these were elderly citizens over fifty years of age. Evenley lost several of its parishioners in this attack, one of which was Mrs. C Shelford, who had mothered all the girls of Evenley School for forty odd years and knew them all from infants. She was surely a grand lady in her work for Evenley.

Mr. C. Shelford retired as Schoolmaster, but continued to play the organ in Evenley Church for several more years and still lived in Evenley.

1920

A new era had begun and an exodus from the land followed. As boys left school, they could not find work on the land as formerly and boys had to leave their homes for work elsewhere, in London and the Midlands where they could learn a trade. Several families emigrated to Canada from the district. One or two boys from Evenley joined the newly formed Royal Air Force, formerly the Flying Corps.

Professional Football and Cricket were in full swing again as the seasons came round and attention was on this in its turn. The local Football and Cricket Clubs were started again and the South Northants Cricket League came into being, of which Evenley Cricket Club was a member, playing their matches at home in the Cricket Field at Evenley Hall.

Most young men now owned a bicycle and a few owned a motor cycle. More and more motor cars were to be seen, owner driven and the pony and trap was on its way off the roads

Hunting with hounds continued with packs and meets as pre-war.

Many of the hunting gentlemen now wore black coats and although a few had hunting pink jackets it was not such a colourful affair as pre 1914.

1921

There was still a shortage of goods in the shops. Boots, shoes and clothing were scarce and of poor quality. The price of beer, tobacco and cigarettes had increased threefold and with these came increases in wages—twenty two shillings a week for farm workers.

Most towns and villages erected their own memorials to the fallen in various shapes and design at this time. Evenley's war memorial stands on the village green and the names of the fallen are to be seen engraved on a brass tablet in Evenley Church.

1922

A new medium was on the air. BBC broadcasting had begun '2 LO' calling. Crystal sets with headphones were being made cheaply and sold to those who cared to buy them, carrying a ten shilling licence fee and soon most homes had their crystal sets, their owners fiddling with a cat's whisker to hear music or talks relayed from London. The Cup Final for Football was commentated on and relayed from Stamford Bridge and aroused great interest in this year.

The year was a great occasion for Brackley and district. The Northamptonshire Agriculture Show was held for two days in Evenley Park, causing great interest among the farming folk. A lighter farm tractor was shown, and soon there were two or three working in the district. They were the first Fordson tractors and they had come to stay. The first Fordson tractor at Evenley was bought and worked on the Evenley Hall Estate Farm.

1923

The transport system had improved and there were now a few buses, privately owned and these ran together with the railways doing cheap and regular trips by train and bus to Banbury, London and elsewhere. Travel was cheap and easy.

A miners' strike caused great hardship early in the year and there was a shortage of coal. Many homes in Evenley and the district suffered in consequence.

In April, 1923, the Rev. Canon Edward Worsley died. He had been Vicar of Evenley for 54 years, a friend to all and had given a lifetime's work to the Church and parishioners of Evenley. The Rev. RC Bates was inducted as Vicar of Evenley in 1923 during November. Sunday School was now held in the Church at 3pm.

A new county modern school having been built at Brackley, Evenley children over eleven years of age were schooled at Brackley, walking into Brackley, taking their lunches with them for the day and the infants from five to eleven were schooled at Evenley by a Schoolmistress. No scripture lessons were now taken by the Vicar in Evenley School.

Mr. C. Shelford resigned as Organist and Choirmaster and choir practice ended in Evenley School. He had been Organist and Choirmaster for fifty two years.

Several of the farms and the Church land were sold at this time and became privately owned at Evenley. There were Rectory Farm, Plomers Firs (Plowman's Furze) Farm, Barley Mow Farm, Astwick Farm and the White House Farm. This land was approximately one third of Evenley Parish's fifteen hundred acres. The sale of these farms brought several changes and they were now owned by dairy farmers and laid down to grass.

Arable had now changed to milk, needing only a skeleton staff of labour as pre 1914. The single farm workers drifted further afield and some of the married men worked on the roads where road work was in progress.

Single girls went further away towards London and the Midlands and many of the larger houses did not employ as many domestic servants as in former years. Chauffeurs, grooms and gardeners were now becoming a luxury and many of the stables of the larger houses carried fewer horses for hunting purposes.

A new type of wireless receiver came out, the loud speaker cabinet and many of these were now selling at about ten pounds and soon the crystal sets with headphones and cat's whiskers were relegated to the dustbin or attic.

1925

Major Allen made alterations to the Malt House Barn and opened it for a Working Men's Club for the benefit of the village, acting as a Village Hall for its meetings and recreation for whist drives, socials and dances. It was a generous amenity for the people of Evenley. This property has become today the village shop and post office.

1926

There had been great industrial unrest in the major industries during the last years and the General Strike followed in 1926. There was a stoppage of work that was felt over the whole country. All the miners, railwaymen and other industries stopped work and others indirectly were thrown out of work. There was chaos in industry, except in agriculture, where the work proceeded, although this was sometimes disrupted. No milk was taken to the stations on the railway and other means had to be found to get the milk away from the farms. The threshing machines were unable to thresh owing to a shortage of steam coal for the steam engines of the contractors who travelled from farm to farm to work and for a time this work was at a standstill and household coal became scarce again.

The farm tractors, although few in numbers in many cases, were now put to work to drive the threshing machines and it was found that they were quite as good as the steam engine for betel work and once started did not require a driver as did the steam engine. It was the beginning of the end. The steam engine had had its day. The General Strike ended. The motor lorry and truck and vans were now coming out on the roads and many firms and companies owned their own vehicles to deliver their goods in large numbers and this began a great loss to the railways.

The milk factory at Buckingham was a depot of the United Dairy Company and the Dairy Company's lorries started to pick up the milk from the farms and took the milk finally to their depots in London.

1926-1930

There was a marked increase of better agricultural machinery during these years at the County Agricultural Shows—petrol and paraffin engines, tractors and ploughs, haymaking machinery and milking machines of various makes and the first milking machine came to Evenley at this time.

Several Dutch barns (an open steel roofed shed) were erected on some of the farms, to store loose hay and straw for feeding, doing away with the job of thatching as formerly it had been stacked in ricks.

1931

The Rev. R.C Bates left Evenley and the Rev. R.W Oakley became Vicar of Evenley.

Train travel to London was cheap and reasonable at this time - twelve shillings a ticket for most trains daily on the Great Central and London, Midland and Scottish Railways. The Midland Red buses started a fairly regular service to Banbury, Buckingham and Northampton.

Great Central Station, Brackley

In the early years of the 1930's the GPO gave Evenley and most of the other villages a telephone kiosk and so organised a public service.

The early years of the 1930's were known as the Hungry Thirties and there was much unemployment throughout the country. Other countries were in much similar circumstances and trade was bad and felt worldwide the meat and livestock markets were at a low ebb and the bottom fell out of the property and land sales and market transactions. Four years 1930 to 1934 were very bad. The price of corn was very low. Eighteen shillings was the average price of wheat per quarter of four and a half hundredweight and it had to be clean and good. Oats and barley were also cheaper—oats twelve shillings per quarter three hundredweight, barley fifteen shillings per quarter four hundredweight. The depression was world wide. 1935 saw a great improvement and gradually things looked brighter for the next few years of the 1930s.

The County Councils put in hand during these years a roads improvement work scheme to widen the major roads and take out many dangerous curves and corners that were in existence at that time. Motor traffic was growing fast in numbers and many accidents, some fatal, took place.

1934

Brackley now had electric house lighting, recently laid by cables from Northampton via Buckingham and now it was brought to Evenley from Brackley. Major WH Allen had it installed in his own property at Evenley Hall, in Evenley Church and in all his cottages for those tenants who wanted it. There were a few aged tenants who seemed afraid of electricity and these kept to their paraffin lamps to the end of their days. This was a real blessing for the mothers at Evenley to have their homes lit by electric light, being cleaner and better in every way and the paraffin oil lamps were relegated to the attics. Electric light was used for the first time at the Harvest Festival Service in Evenley Church in this year.

The Ford Motor Company brought out a new and better model Fordson tractor for £155. One could be obtained for a deposit of £50 and many were sold and fewer horses were needed on the farms.

The Silver Jubilee

King George V's Silver Jubilee took place on May 15th, 1935 and celebrations took place throughout the country. It was a day's holiday for all schoolchildren and Evenley held its own celebration, a collection to help in this having been made from all households in the parish. A good collection of money was made. The day was fine, warm and sunny and Evenley was well decorated with flags and bunting. Most cottages had their Union Jacks and a large Union Jack was flown on the flag pole at Evenley School.

King George V and Queen Mary

Most of the men folk had the whole day off work and the church bells rang out at twelve o'clock. In the afternoon, sports for men, women and children took place, followed by a meat tea for everyone. The children of the village sat down and were served first, the adults sitting down afterwards at a second sitting. There were plenty of helpers and everyone was served to a splendid tea that took place in the Men's Club Room, the Village Hall.

Another peal on the church bells rang out at six thirty and there were more sports into the evening, ending with a tug-of-war for the men, married and single. This was followed by a dance and sing-song in the Village Hall. Refreshments were plenteous, served from a tent on the Green and a most enjoyable day ended for young and old alike. A sum of money being left over from these proceedings, it was decided to buy a teak garden seat and set it up on the Village Green, where it can be seen and used today after nearly forty years' service.

The Squire Dies

At Christmas, 1936 Evenley was stunned by the death of Major WH Allen suddenly at his home at Evenley Hall. He was a good country squire, well liked by the parishioners of Evenley and a good benefactor to the village. In his time he had made many major improvements to the water supply and sewage facilities and he had turned the Malt House Barn into the Men's Club Room for the recreation of the menfolk of Evenley. He was a good churchman and sportsman and keeper of the many fine old oak, elm and beech trees that flourished on the Evenley Hall estate. A well liked country gentleman, difficult to replace.

The sale of the Evenley Hall estate took place by auction at Brackley Town Hall on 26th July 1938 and comprised Evenley Hall, three first class farms and fifty four cottages in an area of 1080 acres. It was sold in ninety four lots. Most of the tenants had had a previous opportunity to acquire their own properties and a few of the tenants of the cottages did so on this date. The cottages that did not sell singly were sold in twos and threes or more in a lump after the sale ended and realised from £75 to £180 each. For a man in work with a family it was a sound investment. The cottages carried a very low rent and had been well maintained, soundly constructed and were in good order inside and out. The rental value varied from £4.10 to £8.10 yearly, but the majority of the cottages were rented at £5.13.4 yearly, with an extra charge of five shillings yearly for electrical fittings and had remained unaltered from pre war times. Water was included for each cottage.

The village water supply was sold where it stood, together with the plot of ground, wind and electrically driven pump and fittings as a single unit to a new owner.

The school and school house, rented to the Northamptonshire County Council, with a 99 years lease almost finished, had a few more years to run and the Village Green was to be sold in time.

Evenley Hall with its parklands, timber and water supply came into the hands of the trustees of the National Children's Home and the three farms also had new owners. The Evenley Hall estate was broken up and was now occupied by a large number of new tenants as owner occupiers.

Changes were taking place in farming. Milk was being produced and sent by train, some of it to London, but the bulk to Birmingham Milk Factory, where it was processed and made into chocolate.

A new breed of sheep, the Border Leicester, was being bred and these finally took the place of the Oxford and Hampshire Downs flocks. These had to be penned on the land with hurdles and were in them all winter. They had to be washed and cleaned up in the spring. The Border Leicester were more suited as a grass sheep and did not get dirty as the other breeds and did not require washing prior to shearing and so the washing of the sheep ended.

Most farmers now had a power hay turner, side delivery rake, tedder, elevator to help with the hay. The hand rake and pitch fork were going, as other things had gone. The self binder was in general use on the farms, horse drawn as yet. The tractor had not yet arrived to speed up the harvest. There was for most farms a petrol engine for many jobs, pumping water, pulping roots, driving elevators and other stationary jobs. Many of the older horses were brought back from France and billeted with a driver, a wounded soldier, to work on the farms in pairs where they would be required.

A Sign in the Sky

In the autumn of 1938, the Aurora Borealis or Northern Lights was seen all over the country. It was as if the whole sky in a north westerly direction was on fire - a most unusual sight for this part of the country and in some quarters it was said to be an omen to herald a war in which England would be involved. The Aurora Borealis has not been seen since in like manner.

THE SECOND WORLD WAR

Other writers have told of the causes and progress of this war. Most cities, towns and villages had their own war time accounts of events that took place in England between 1939 and 1945, some of which were unrecorded and have been forgotten altogether. No homes were safe and every man, woman and child in the country became vulnerable to attack by bombs, shells and missiles of all kinds.

Perhaps the first of many war time restrictions was a complete blackout of the whole country. No lights were to be shown from windows and doors from any building or dwelling after dusk. Motor vehicles, bikes etc. had to get their headlamps shaded to direct the light on the road in front. The rear red lights were unaffected. Fires in fields, allotments and gardens were made during daylight hours, to be put out at dusk. The careless flashing of lamps and torches was frowned upon. This was work for the Special Constabulary and Police, by giving a quiet warning at first and later on, if lights were shown, followed by a summons and a fairly heavy fine. The RAF made several flights over the country during the hours of darkness and reported that it was a good blackout for the whole country.

Bill as a Special Constable

All men in the Reserves of any armed services had to report for service. There were two such men that lived at Evenley. Three other Evenley men were already serving in the RAF and so five Evenley men saw service in war from the beginning.

Children were evacuated from London and other large cities and the Brackley district took a goodly number from London into a fresh home, some of them coming to Evenley.

Identity cards and gas masks were issued to all, as air raids were expected. All men and single women from eighteen to forty five were registered for national service and a census of all farm animals and heavy machinery, tractors, vehicles etc. was taken.

The Phoney War

The first six months of the war were fairly quiet for the countryside and it was being called a Phoney War. German aircraft were making their appearance in daylight over England in small numbers and sometimes, when the day was clear could be seen flying at a great height. The sound that came from the engines of the German aircraft was very different from that of the British aircraft, which had a steadier drone and rhythm, very distinct and noticeable. One or two instances of bombs being dropped were reported, but very little damage was done. Air Raid Sirens were installed at all the fire stations in the country.

Firefighters in Brackley

The invasion of England was now expected and preparations for meeting it quickly took place. Bodies of men in every town and village were enrolled to make up the Home Guard into a fighting force and to strengthen the ambulance and fire services. All the road signs of towns and villages, directional signs of all kinds were taken up by the County Councils. Place names on all vehicles were painted out. People were told to travel long distances by train if possible, not to discuss the names of places with strangers and to stay near their homes and work at all times. Many kinds of obstacles were placed in many of the large fields to prevent landings from aircraft.

The Blitz

On November 15th, 1940, the night after the Blitz on Coventry, the villagers of Evenley had a narrow escape and a fright from a string of nineteen bombs that fell in the fields near the Mixbury Road, crossing the village and ending in a field off the Oxford to Brackley road, the A43.

One bomb fell into the gardens close to Evenley Hall farmhouse, a second fell into gardens fifty yards from Evenley Church, killing nine cows and injuring fifteen others in a herd of thirty two. The cows that were found alive afterwards were in a sorry plight; they were afraid to move. The grass field they laid in was smothered in loose stones and the hedgerow looked as though it had been threshed and gnawed by rabbits. None of the cows had been directly hit by the bomb. They all appeared to have had a terrible stoning. Apart from some ceilings cracked in the cottages and windows cracked and slates shaken off, there was no other damage done. This was Evenley's major incident during the war years. There were other bombs dropped later on near Evenley, but these only made holes in the ground with very little damage.

In 1941 there was a great call up of men and women for the armed forces and many men and women who joined were taken into the RAF. Others were taken for the Army, Navy and the Women's Land Army (WLA). Evenley, like other places lost its men.

Many of the large mansions and country houses that were vacant were commandeered at this time, including Evenley Hall and Brackley House. Others in the neighbourhood were occupied by the Army.

The telephone wires that ran overhead along the roadside were taken down and laid underground. A long line of ammunition sheds were erected on the verge of the A43 Northampton to Oxford road. Emergency food supplies were set up and stored in most places. All tramps were picked up, also gypsies and escorted off the roads and crowds were forbidden in dance halls and other public places.

The bombing of London continued with Bristol, Bath and Plymouth and other cities getting their share indiscriminately—bombs everywhere.

On December 11th, 1941, Evenley had another tremendous explosion. A landmine had fallen in Evenley Allotments, near the Buckingham to Banbury road. It made a crater sixty feet wide and forty feet deep and pieces of rock weighing fifty six to a hundred and twelve pounds were picked up half a mile away. No other damage was done, apart from blocking the road with stones and rubble.

The making and building of new airfields went on very fast in the district and the town of Brackley was ringed by airfields in South Northamptonshire and North Oxfordshire—Finmere, Croughton, Hinton-in-the-Hedges, Turweston, Silverstone and Chipping Warden and others in the Banbury district. At first these airfields were flying training grounds, but as the war went on most became operational.

The railways that had started to decline now showed a large surge upwards in railway traffic. The RAF personnel and the goods for making the airfields from Brackley station made the railways busy again.

At the end of the war, in 1945, all the men and women from Evenley who had served in the forces came home safely, unlike World War I. The village of Evenley suffered no fatal casualties, and this was something to be ever thankful for, after all that England had gone through during World War II.

During the Second World War a machinery depot was set up in Evenley by the War Agricultural Committee to help farmers in their work and it continued for a time after the war; these depots did good work for agriculture, being supplied with all the latest farm machinery. They had tractors, ploughs, harrows, cultivators, drills and finally combines and balers.

The combine harvesters had come to stay, to the detriment of the other threshing machines of pre war times and rubber tyres were so improved for tractors that they now had standard equipment tyres of this type. The war had brought many inventions for farming, building and other purposes, including the diesel engine and electric motor. To see a horse working on the farms was now almost a thing of the past. Horse work had now almost disappeared in this area.

The value in land and property was now almost double and appeared to be going up very fast and more and more people from the towns and cities were buying their own house or cottage in the country districts.

POST WAR YEARS

In 1946 and 1947 housing for renting purposes had become a problem for the whole area and the Rural District Council decided on a building programme to build new houses in most of the villages in South Northamptonshire according to the needs and size of places. Nine council houses were built in Evenley at this time.

The church bells that had been silenced more or less since the war were now considered to be unsafe for ringing and most of the ringers had died, so the art of bell ringing was lost at Evenley.

Flying had made such progress that people were now flying abroad for their holidays and flying from one continent to another was commonplace.

Although these changes and events refer to my own native village of Evenley, a lot of them could be equally applied to any other place in the Brackley district, or the South Northamptonshire—North Oxfordshire area during the past sixty five years.

PICTURES FROM THE PAST

There are pictures that stand out clearly in my mind during my early years.

The Shelswell Coach 1904 to 1906

The Shelswell Estate coach, making its way to and from Brackley, passed through Evenley. There it was, a lovely covered-in four wheel coach on solid rubber tyres, being drawn by four magnificent horses in black and shining harness, driven by its coachman sitting high on its front open seat and on a seat at the same level at the back sat the footman, with travelling cases on the top of the coach in front of him. These men were dressed in hunting pink tunics, white breeches and black silk top hat with a cockade to identify the two and both wore black hunting boots with long laced tops. On either side of the coach ran one or two large dogs, probably Great Danes, level with the doors of the coach and inside were the occupants and owners of the cavalcade. The village children were scared when these massive long legged dogs whistled by and they quickly got out of the way.

The Ploughing Match 1908 to 1911

The district Ploughing Match and Hedge Cutting Competition was held at Evenley during these years in the first two fields from Evenley crossroads on the right hand side of the road leading to Charlton, known as the White Post and Sanfoin Ground. I was taken to this by my father and there were many spectators to see the quality of the work done and to give their opinions as to who were doing the best work and, I suppose, to help drink some of the ale that went with such functions.

I was too young to be interested in the ploughing, but the setting is as clear in my mind as it was then. A lovely sunny autumn day with Brackley Town shining in the distance. On the right were those splendid beech trees leading into Brackley in all their russet leaves and autumn glory. There were the white beer tents and the ploughmen, ploughs and horses ploughing their own piece of land they had drawn for in lots before starting work. Each team had to plough half an acre in four and a half hours, points being awarded for the starting, laying and finishing of the furrows and the same thing applied to the hedge cutting competition, where each competitor was to lay, stake and bind eleven yards of hedge in four and a half hours. The first prize for ploughing was a new horse plough for the owner of the plough team and a money prize, first, second and third for the ploughman and hedge cutters. These prizes were given by the implement makers and tradesmen of the whole district.

There were the spectators walking and watching from the headlands and the judges in their white coats inspecting the work as it proceeded and the ploughmen, stripped in a clean white shirt, each trying to go as straight as the next man, with the greensward of clover aftermath being turned over well nigh perfect.

A team of magnificent horses took my fancy. They looked like twins; their colour of dappled grey and black spots were so much alike that they seemed to me to stand out well in front of all the rest of the teams and the only sounds to be heard were a gentle word of command from the ploughmen and the snorting of the horses as they walked to and fro across the field, enjoying every minute of it, seemingly.

The tractor today will be ever unable to make such a picture or even show such good work as these ploughmen, for they only rush through the job nowadays—called progress!

The Guards Band at Tusmore Park

In 1905 there was a great occasion at Tusmore Park, for what I could never understand. It may have been the centenary of the Battle of Trafalgar, because it was the home of the Earl of Effingham and he was more or less in command of the Royal Navy at the time of Trafalgar or rather one of his ancestors.

Again I was taken by my father to this celebration, being carried on his shoulders to Tusmore Park. A considerable crowd from Evenley walked the distance and after waiting at Evenley cross roads for some time, yes, they could be heard. They were coming.

It was the Grenadier or Coldstream Guards, marching with their band playing on their way to Tusmore Park from Brackley Great Central Railway station. It was a lovely sunny day and everyone that could walk or go by pony trap was gathering at the turn to see the Guardsmen go by and a big crowd had gathered on the verge underneath the beech trees close by. The sound of their music could be heard as they marched down through Brackley. What a grand sight it was to see these men as they came into view, such giants in their bearskin hats. It was my first close up view of the Guards in full dress, red tunics, blue trousers with their red stripes and those shining boots and buttons, a wonderful sight for a painter, surely. After the Guardsmen had passed by, the crowd of people followed behind them to Tusmore Park. It was also my first visit to

Tusmore.

As soon as they arrived at Tusmore the Guardsmen lined each side of the arched gateway, still playing their instruments and the crowd of people passed through them into Tusmore Park. Inside the Park were several tents and in front of these were seats for the Guardsmen and music stands all ready for them to sit and play for the occasion. The white stone lion on the arched gateway overhead, as clean and white as snow to complete a picture that I could never forget. But later on in years, when I recalled this to my father, he said he could not remember what was going on at Tusmore at that time, but said he could remember the Guardsmen all right.

I thought I must be dreaming too, but no, there was a man living at Juniper until a short time ago, some ten years older than I was and he remembered the occasion as I had done and he told me it was the centenary of the Battle of Trafalgar that had been celebrated at Tusmore Park.

The Night Sky 1909

It was given out in school that a comet would be visible to the naked eye during the spring or early summer nights of this year. All the eyes of the young men or the older boys looked into the night sky to see if they could see it, scanning the stars like astronomers every night, for no one of my generation had ever seen one, a star with a long tail. A crowd of men and boys stood watching at the School Corner. Many did not know where or what to look for. It would be seen high in the sky in a south westerly direction over Croughton.

After several weeks of watching had passed by and some of us had given it up as a bad job, a few boys of my age were looking and searching the stars on this particular night, when suddenly one boy, my school pal, said "I can see it!" and he promptly dashed off to inform our schoolmaster. Yes there it was. The star with the long tail could be seen quite plainly with the naked eye and through binoculars and if my memory is correct, it was only to be seen again on the following night and a comet has not been seen since with the naked eye.

This was a memorable year for me. I was taken in to the Evenley

Church Choir and so became its junior choir boy.

The Army Manoeuvres 1913

It was given out in the press that army manoeuvres would take place in the Midlands during the summer of 1913. During September and October, when the harvest had neared completion, there was great activity by the Army in the Midland counties, moving around from place to place with horses and service wagons and the clatter of horses' hooves was heard from daylight to dusk for several weeks. At night the troops were camped in tents in the large parklands of the neighbourhood.

It was during this time that the second aeroplane was seen on the ground near Evenley. It had landed in a field known as the South Barn Ground on Plomers Firs Farm, about half a mile from Evenley crossroads. Soon the field was full of folk coming in from all directions on foot, as it was inaccessible from the roadways. The police were soon there and a rope was put around it to keep the spectators from touching it. The plane was an army biplane and had landed after losing its bearings. It was guarded by the police all night and in the morning flew away again. There was great excitement in all this and the question was asked "What did it all mean?" Then for a while it was quickly forgotten.

The Northern Lights, the Aurora Borealis, were seen several nights during the autumn months of 1913 and there were folks who said there was a war coming.

Christmas was not far away and 1913 passed away as most other years had done, but little did folks know that it was the last peaceful Christmas they would know for some time.

The Blizzard of 1917

During the month of April, 1917 there was a terrific blizzard, starting with a snowstorm in the afternoon and continuing during the whole of the night. Great damage was done. Slates and tiles were torn off the houses and many of Evenley's fine old elm and beech trees were uprooted. Three elms were uprooted near the school in a heap and many beech trees were uprooted on the Oxford road into Brackley and many more in Evenley Park and district. The telephone wires were blown down all around and when these were repaired, the GPO put the telephone into all the village post offices of the district, including Evenley.

The Coronation of King George V

The Coronation of King George V took place in 1911. There was great rejoicing all over the country and every place celebrated the occasion.

Evenley had its own celebration. Every house in the village hung out its flags - the Union Jack. It was on occasions like this that the school flag was to be seen flying on the school flagpole. Clean as a new pin, there it was, one of two large flags of the same size, five feet by three feet six and the other was flying on a house that also had a flagpole next to the School House. Both poles had been newly painted for the occasion. The church bells rang out merrily and Evenley let itself go. It was decorated as well as I ever saw it. There were several tents erected in a field near the school known as Lawyers Close. There was a beer tent, tea tent and a tent laid out with tables and chairs to sit down to a lovely spread of cold meat and all the salads in profusion. Everyone sat down in their turn.

Evenley had to my best recollection a population of between 300 and 400 at this time. However, all had what they needed. Sports were begun, racing for men and women, boys and girls; throwing the cricket ball, obstacle races, threading the needle, egg and spoon races, the lot, one after another. There was a tug-of-war, married versus single. There were plenty of strong men living at Evenley and plenty of men who liked a strong pint of beer. The ale was strong in those days and what with the fizzy lemonade and ginger beer for the women and children, the refreshments were served free by the publican of the Red Lion, who remained at Evenley for long afterwards. A good day was enjoyed by all who were there and that included the squire and parson of Evenley, the farmers and tradesmen and the smallest child who could run. All were invited. And the cost - well the whole village contributed in some way or another.

Things were much the same at Brackley and finished with a firework display. Some of the rockets that exploded high in the air could be seen at Evenley. I was there to see it.

Evenley folk had had their celebrations and were anxious to hear how things had gone in Westminster Abbey. It seemed as though the newspaper folk had anticipated this, for the next morning a boy came up from Brackley - yes, on a bicycle with a load of papers, crying "Paper, a penny" and with every paper was a souvenir copy of the Coronation. The boy quickly sold his papers and he was given an order "Bring me one tomorrow". So Evenley now had a daily paper delivered to the door by bicycle in the same manner as today.

APPENDIX
EVENLEY PARISH

Evenley parish is one of the largest in South Northamptonshire and consists of approximately 3200 acres, nearly twice the area of the parish of Brackley. It lies in the southernmost corner of Northamptonshire and joins the counties of Buckinghamshire and Oxfordshire at a place marked on the ordnance map as Three Shires Pit on the river Ouse. It leaves Buckinghamshire here, the parish and county boundary continuing bow shaped across Mixbury to Evenley road to the Bowling Green, taking a sharp right hand turn and continues again bow shaped to the A43, clearly marked today Oxfordshire on one side of the road and Northamptonshire on the other. The boundary takes a sharp left hand turn here on the A43, which is now in Oxfordshire and continues alongside the road, bow shaped slightly past White House Cottages to Ockley Brook.

This is the parish and county boundary going towards Croughton and on towards Aynho parish. This brook and others on the western side of the A43, from a spot near Evenley crossroads to the Barley Mow drains into the Thames.

The parish boundary leaves the county boundary, Ockley Brook at a spot known years ago as Kankum and divides the parish of Croughton from Evenley awkwardly and cuts the RAF base in half, with the largest number of acres in Evenley parish and rightly should be known as RAF Evenley and Croughton. This part of the parish boundary is now lost from Kankum to Astwick Farm. There are very few men alive today who know where it is.

The parish boundary can be found, enclosing Astwick Farm and

Plomers Firs Farm in an almost straight line to the Hinton-in-the-Hedges, Croughton and Evenley crossroads.

The boundary winds back right to Edge Corner and leaves the Charlton—Evenley road on the left, winding round via Black Jack Spinney and Cuttle Brook and joining the river Ouse on the south west of Brackley, winding to the A43 and continuing on for half a mile where the river Ouse picks up another tributary from Whitfield, Turweston and Brackley Mill, not very far from Brackley Parish Church. Once again it forms the parish and county boundary between Buckinghamshire and Northamptonshire, then winds along meadow land under the now disused railway bridges of the LMS and Great Central Railways. Then it joins up again at Three Shires Pit in the river Ouse where this story started. What a walk it would make!

This large parish was halved roughly from the Mixbury boundary, running in line and enclosing Evenley village and going on to the Evenley crossroads and up towards Charlton at Hinton crossroads. On the north side of this line was the Evenley Hall estate and on the south side the Church Lands estate and this ran into North Oxfordshire cutting a large slice of land between the Shelswell estate and Aynho Park estate. This part of the county was cut up in this manner and all this part of the county was farmed and worked by the horse.

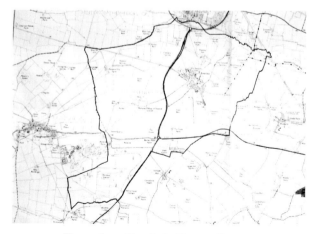

Evenley Parish Boundary

BRACKLEY

It could be said that what went on at Brackley affected the neighbouring villages. All were interwoven with agriculture and all were like a large family.

Brackley market for livestock and its shops sold all the necessary things for life. There were no real industry or factories in Brackley. There were two breweries that employed a large number of workers. It had good schools and two railway stations that gave good connections with all parts of the country. It was agriculture that found most of the work indirectly for the people living in the Brackley district and its workers were like brothers, in as much as they all knew one another for miles around.

Evenley was closely connected with Brackley, being separated only by Evenley Park lands and is so today. St. Peter's Church, with its six bells was its chief place of worship and was well attended in these years at Brackley. It had a Methodist Chapel and its Salvation Army Citadel and Band.

Brackley too had a good brass band, the Town Band and also a strong troop of Boy Scouts. One or two boys came into this from Evenley. Brackley also had its Mayor and Corporation.

THE VILLAGE TODAY

As with all villages, Evenley has evolved still further since these two personal memoirs were written and will continue to do so. The village has grown, the inhabitants come and go more frequently and travel more widely and local employment is less rural. But perhaps no changes will ever be quite so momentous as those that took place in the 20th century. The memoirs of those who lived through those times serve to remind us of that unique part of history and how it affected Evenley.

Also published by Evenley Residents Association

ASPECTS OF EVENLEY

This book tells the story of Evenley,
a small village in Northamptonshire.
from pre Roman times to the present day.

It shows how it has developed over time,
has been shaped by its past and finishes with
a suggested walk around the village

This book and

TALES OF EVENLEY

are for sale for £7.95 at

EVENLEY VILLAGE SHOP

+44 (0)1280 702452

www.evenley.info

or

BY POST
from

Evenley Residents Association
Fairfield, Church Lane, Evenley, Brackley, NN13 5SG

Price £10 sterling payable in advance to include p. & p.